Infinity and Zebra Stripes:

Life with Gifted Children

Wendy Skinner

D1403472

Great Potential Press™

Infinity and Zebra Stripes: Life with Gifted Children

Copy editing: Jennifer Ault
Interior design: The Printed Page
Cover design: Hutchinson-Frey

Published by Great Potential Press, Inc.
P.O. Box 5057
Scottsdale, AZ 85261

Printed on recycled paper

11 10 09 08 07   5 4 3 2 1

Names of individuals in this book have been changed to protect identities.

==

Library of Congress Cataloging-in-Publication Data

Skinner, Wendy, 1961-
  Infinity and zebra stripes : life with gifted children / Wendy Skinner.
    p. cm.
  ISBN-13: 978-0-910707-81-7 (pbk.)
  ISBN-10: 0-910707-81-2 (pbk.)
  1. Gifted children. 2. Child rearing. 3. Gifted children—Psychology. 4.
Parenting. I. Title. II. Title: Raising highly gifted children.
  HQ773.5.S545 2007
  306.874087'9—dc22
                              2007014278

# Dedication

This book is for my mother, Betty Johnson, whose life work has guided and encouraged thousands of children, including me, to follow their dreams.

Acknowledgments

Books, like people, do not develop and mature without the encouragement and support of others. I am thankful to all those who read the manuscript at various stages, to those who gave me their expertise and wisdom, and to those whose compassion helped me through the rough spots. Some of the most notable of these are Karilyn Jons, Ann Haines, Joe Pastoor, Karen Peterson, Deborah Ruf, Debra Kass Orenstein, and Stuart Dansinger. I also want to thank my beloved writing colleagues whom I met through The Loft Literary Center in Minneapolis, Minnesota, including Mary Jean Port, Nancy Raeburn, Larry Storey, Naomi Rettke, and Alison Bergblom Johnson. Everyone involved in the Minnesota Council for Gifted and Talented should likewise know how much I have appreciated their important work. A special endearing thank you goes to Jo Henriksen and Joan Brinkman, whose talents and spirits are irreplaceable.

I would also like to thank Janet Gore and Jim Webb for their editing expertise and kindness, and Great Potential Press for taking a chance on me and our story.

Finally, I am ever grateful to my husband and my parents for believing in the story and the stories of thousands of others like us. And, without whom this story would be naught, I give my warmest of hugs to my son and daughter.

Contents

 Preface

> "...I don't really have anyone I'm comfortable talking with about this. I always feel guilty if I mention that my 14-year-old son is taking a college math class, because other parents just can't relate."
> ~Beth, mother of three gifted children

Beth sums it up well. Her feelings of isolation, secrecy, and sometimes guilt illustrate what thousands of other parents of gifted and talented children experience. We have to go underground. We feel that our stories are so personal, so intimate, or so often peculiar to the ordinary person that no one could possibly understand us. It's as if we're strangers from another planet.

Have you ever experienced a reaction of disbelief when someone hears you mention inadvertently that your first-grade child, for example, is reading—on her own—C.S. Lewis' Narnia series? "No way!" the other person says (or thinks) in astonishment and skepticism. Or, "How do you do it?" as if seeking a secret formula from you. "My fourth-grader is struggling in reading!"

It only takes one or two uncomfortable encounters like this for a parent of a gifted child to censor herself in public and share stories of her children only within her own family—and sometimes not even there.

Yet if every parent of a gifted child reacts by keeping silent, no one will ever know that there is a whole world of us out here! Parents of gifted children need each other as peers, friends, and counselors to share our worries, concerns, and frustrations, as well as our pleasure and elation. By speaking up, we can find each other and discover that each of us is not an isolated island, but rather one of many islands in an archipelago, facing the relentless waves of the sea of popular culture together. By connecting with other parents through the tradition of storytelling, we gain a deeper understanding and appreciation of our own situations.

The purpose of this book is to share my family's story, which is only one of many stories about being a parent of unusual children. It's a story of one set of parents who struggle, and eventually succeed, in working hand-in-hand with teachers and administrators to meet the needs of their two exceptionally gifted children in the public school system.

Many elements of this story will be familiar to all parents—treasured memories of delightful discoveries and unexpected surprises. There are also stories of frustrating barriers, dogged persistence towards goals, and feelings of relief and celebration that follow each success, no matter how small.

I hope our story will bring hope to all parents, whether or not their child has a label of "gifted." All children need and deserve their parents' advocacy as they navigate the classrooms and philosophies of schools.

Introduction

My husband and I had very different upbringings. Growing up in the suburbs of Minneapolis with three older siblings, I was the spoiled youngest child until I was 10, when my little sister was born. My husband was the oldest of two, and only 10 months older than his sister. Growing up in a small farming community on the eastern plains of Colorado, he always took the role of the responsible oldest child.

Whether it is in the genes, the environment, or the magical mix of both, gifted children are usually born into families with gifted parents. So it was with us. And people manifest their talents in a variety of ways. Our two sets of parents are examples of this.

My father was a research physicist by day but spent many hours at his desk at night studying global climatology. He later became an adjunct professor of geology at the University of Minnesota. My mother was involved in local politics and government, and she sat on numerous boards, including the historical society and a children's theater company. She also served on the Minnesota Council for the Gifted and Talented and founded a summer school for gifted children.

My husband's father was a highly skilled auto mechanic and became the prized technician for a handful of professional drag car racing teams, one of which held several national records. He was an avid collector of classic cars and knew every bit of trivia about every model automobile ever made. My husband's mother, a top-notch hairdresser, was a very independent woman who owned her own beauty shop. The family was musically talented; Brian's mother, aunt, uncle, and grandfather were all amateur or professional musicians and performed throughout Eastern Colorado. In addition to music, the family seemed gifted with humor, and gut-splitting hilarity was ever present. Clearly, there were numerous bright, competent people in our family tree.

Brian and I met in college in Colorado. He was studying business, and I was majoring in elementary education and Spanish. Whereas everyone in my family had attended college, Brian was the first in his family to go to college and, unlike me, supported himself both financially and emotionally during his college years. We met at a friend's house party, married a few years later, and moved to Minneapolis-St. Paul.

When our children came along, it was important to us to provide our own primary care for them. Because of my desire, experience with children, and flexibility, I fit the role best. We were more dependent financially on Brian's career in commercial real estate. I could work around family more easily than he with day and nighttime teaching jobs. We felt very fortunate to be able to have one of us stay at home when our first child, Ben, was born and again when our second child, Jillian, came along.

I kept basic records from the day Ben was born, and then, beginning around his first birthday (perhaps when my own sleep deprivation had subsided), I began a detailed journal of my parenting experiences and those of my children as they grew. These writings were essential in recalling the raw details upon which most of this book is based. As you read, you will see how we discovered that we had two rapid learners who required accommodations in their education. They were advanced in certain areas when compared with other children their age; in other areas, they were similar. It was frustrating at first, working with the schools to get the appropriate challenge and acceleration of curriculum, but as time went on, we were able to build a positive relationship of mutual trust. Our approach was that we were all working toward whatever would be best for the specific traits of our children. And through positive communication with school staff, we were fortunate to be able to get the services that our children needed.

If I relied on memory alone, I might have diminished how unusual or challenging our experiences were. My records and writings remind me, however, that our experiences at the time were very real struggles that ultimately (and fortunately) led to very real positive outcomes. Of course we made some mistakes, but we learned from them. Perhaps our experiences in parenting and advocating for our two gifted children will help other parents who face similar challenges.

—Wendy Skinner

 Prologue

Our very bright young son was just seven years old. We had just recently moved him to a new school because he was bored and unhappy in his other school. Now he was happy and excited about learning again.

He always fell asleep late, seeming to need less sleep than the rest of us. One night early in March, his brain was going full strength until nearly midnight. He had just seen a "Bill Nye the Science Guy" television show featuring the topic of evolution. Math was his favorite subject, and he also had been thinking lately about the concepts of zero and infinity. That night, those concepts collided in his brain with fireworks.

Thump. Pad, pad, pad. His dad and I could hear his foot-steps while we lay under the covers reading. I checked the clock. It was 11:28 P.M.

Knock, knock, knock. "Come in, Ben," my husband said. Ben opened our bedroom door and crawled up on our bed with a sheepish grin.

"Can I tell you something?" he asked. He scooted up close to us on his knees. "I know I'm supposed to be in bed, but this is going to keep me up until five in the morning!"

"Go ahead, Ben," I said with a sleepy smile. "If it will keep you up until five in the morning, it must be pretty fantastic. What is it?"

His voice reflected everything from profound awe to giddy celebration. He began with negative numbers and the number one.

"You know you can always get back to one no matter where you are. You could be at negative 10 and add 11 and you'd get one. You could be at negative 1,000,000 and add 1,000,001 and you'd get one. You can *always* get back to one." Here he paused. "Now, how about infinity? You can never, ever, ever, *ever* get to infinity. You can always get to one, but you can never get to infinity. Even if you take infinity minus 10 and add 10 back in, you can't get back to infinity. You just can't because infinity is infinity!"

Ben's enthusiasm swelled. "But now look at nature. Two plus five equals seven. Two plus five will *always* be seven. But black and white zebra stripes won't *always* be black and white. In a billion years they'll be different because of infinite evolutionary adaptations," Ben whooped.

"And when a second passes in time, it never comes again. And if you could put a monitor on a second to keep track of it when it passes—even though you can't, but if you *could*—you could never see it again. And if someone were to count for their whole lifetime, they'd never end, and if their son counted from *his* whole lifetime, *he'd* never end. All because of infinity!"

His excitement was palpable. He was definitely not sleepy. He had been thinking about this and just had to share it with us. We shared his excitement about infinity, zebra stripes, and all the rest. This was truly fun.

Eventually I escorted Ben back to bed, but not before he made sure that we understood every detail of his discoveries. When I returned to our bedroom, Brian and I just looked at each other with eyebrows raised and big smiles on our faces. I leaped back into the bed laughing and pulled the covers back up. "This kid," I said between chuckles, "has got to have more challenge in mathematics than adding five plus five."

This was our son. We enjoyed his love of learning. For a few years, we struggled over finding the right school for him. His younger sister is also highly gifted and different from her age peers.[1] Although the two children are very different, our experiences with Ben helped us know what to do for Jillian.

I think that all parents of gifted children will relate to the joys and struggles we went through. And I think that all teachers will be interested in reading about the school examples and how we worked—sometimes more successfully than other times—with teachers and administration using a teamwork model, not a pushy parent model, to appropriately accommodate our children's educational needs in the classroom.

 Chapter 1

A Turning Point

This was our fourth school conference, and it was only the middle of October. As I sat in the tiny chair with my knees bumping the edge of the low round table, I thought maybe this time we could get moving on a concrete plan for Ben. His experience in first grade up to this point had been totally lacking in any sort of academic challenge, especially in math. It was academically inadequate in other areas as well, but my biggest concern was math. My bright child was struggling against a tide of unending repetition of concepts he had mastered long ago, like counting, simple addition, and subtraction.

"There have to be other children Ben could group with for math so that he can work on something more challenging," I insisted as I switched my gaze from Mrs. Jansen, the gifted and talented teacher, to Señora Cruz, his classroom teacher. "He's been able to do what you're doing now in first-grade math for two or three years. He even wrote last week that his academic goal for first grade was to learn division."

Señora Cruz's dark eyes met mine as she shrugged her tiny shoulders and replied, "I don't think there are any other students who would be ready to do what Ben may be ready to do in math."

"What do you mean? There must be *someone*," I said. I turned to the gifted teacher. "Didn't you test some others in his grade that he could group with for math?"

"Well," Mrs. Jansen paused awkwardly, "I really don't think so, actually."

"Can I clarify something here?" I was beginning to understand that I must have been missing something. Why would it be so difficult to group Ben with others like him for math? "How exactly *did* Ben score on the tests compared to the other kids?"

Mrs. Jansen replied in a quiet voice, "Ben had the highest score in the school. He had the highest score of all the first graders in the district."

My eyes glazed over momentarily. Had I heard correctly?

That October conference with Ben's first-grade teacher and the gifted education teacher was my big wakeup call. For the first time, I was presented with a concrete example of just how different Ben was academically, at least in mathematics, compared to his first-grade peers. From that brief part of our discussion, I realized that I was dealing with a much more complicated situation than I had anticipated. Addressing the special needs and consequences of Ben's differences would not be simple or easy from this point on. There could be no more playing the "wait-and-see-what-happens" game at school. Ben needed immediate help, and I was the only one who seemed to recognize the urgency in this. It was up to me to come to his aid.

That afternoon marked the beginning of many complex and often intense conferences with school personnel and the school's educational psychologist. It was also the formal beginning of my own education about gifted children. At that dumbfounding moment in Ben's classroom, I knew that a door had just opened for Ben—a door that he had been pounding on for the last year or so. I could no longer avoid the fact that I needed to learn more about parenting and understanding Ben and, for that matter, his younger sister Jillian. They both needed me to advocate for them in the public arena that lay outside the safety and comfort of our own little family. And, simply by fate of being the first born, Ben would be the first to venture through this complex maze of the early school years with me as his rookie guide. The goal was to find a place where he and his sister could learn and grow with a sense of belonging and happiness rather than a sense of alienation and despair.

Cherry-Flavored Cars

The earliest years with Ben were delightful. My pregnancy was uneventful, with no adverse health concerns. After eight hours of labor, Ben entered the world, arriving at 2:34 in the afternoon and weighing a healthy seven pounds, two and a half ounces. At first I credited his calm demeanor to the effects of medication given during labor, but over time, he proved that his relaxed disposition was for the long run.

I attended a new mothers' education class in the maternity wing of the hospital. The class demonstrated basic newborn care for the new mothers, and the instructor chose Ben for her model in how to bathe the baby. He stayed quiet, calm, and content, with wide-open eyes and not a sound from his tiny lips. He seemed acutely aware of his surroundings while the large, adept hands of the maternity nurse lathered up his little head and bathed the rest of his body.

Right from the beginning, people commented how lucky I was and how easy I had it with Ben. He wasn't colicky; he was happy, curious, and had no tantrums like some of the other babies we knew. In the early childhood classes, he began to expose himself to higher levels of socialization around the other mobile toddlers, and he could either initiate or avoid interaction. As young as five months, he liked to explore with other babies and would quietly and carefully watch those around him. Later he experimented by imitating the actions of those other babies and young toddlers. He seemed to be interested in methodically challenging himself.

He sat by himself at six months and walked at 10 months. His relatively early locomotion allowed him to participate alongside the other older babies and toddlers and increase his knowledge of the world. He no longer had to rely on me or Brian to take him where he wanted to go when he had the urge to explore. If he got bored playing with the pile of wooden blocks, he had the freedom to abandon them for the stacking cups across the room or for the pots and pans in the lower kitchen cupboard.

Ben was my traveling buddy for those first three years. He went with me everywhere, and we had a stream of conversation longer than the Mississippi River. Rides in the car were filled with ceaseless discussions, children's song tapes, and "I spy in my little eye" searching games. Walks with Ben strapped onto my back in the carrier were constant field trips of discovery. Every street sign, tree leaf, and roadside dandelion received special examination and analysis. It seemed to me that he always could "talk," and I rarely had a difficult time understanding him, either before or after he spoke actual words.

When he did begin talking, it was in great leaps. As if a neuron had bridged the last remaining gap, in an instant Ben went from two-word phrases to complete three- or more word sentences. Instead of saying, "Car, go," he'd say, "I want the car to go to the grocery store...now!" Once he broke out of the two-word pattern of speech, his sentences seemed unlimited. The articulation of his speech took strangers by surprise in the grocery store or the bakery. His deliberate choice of words, sentence structure, accompanying eye contact, and gestures were unexpectedly precise and sophisticated. He developed a thoughtful and logical approach using language to identify objects. Birds were not "birdies." He distinguished between grackles, robins, and house sparrows. "Grackle" was one of Ben's first words before he was nine months old and was used to identify no other bird but a grackle. And he could specifically identify many other birds.

Ben loved to talk and to play with language. One day early in September when he was nearly two years old, we were out for our daily morning walk and stopped to sit on a favorite rock in the warmth of the ripe summer sunshine. This large rock had been placed on the corner of a quiet neighborhood intersection to prevent winter snowplows from edging too close to the lawns. I sat Ben on top of the boulder, and together we began naming the colors of the cars as they passed. "Green, blue, dark blue, white," we recited methodically. Then, as a red car passed, Ben beat me to the naming and shouted out, "Cherry!" From that point on, the game changed to naming the flavors of the cars and debating which shade of green or blue made a car lime or apple, blueberry or grape.

For nearly two and a half years, Ben and I took part in early childhood family education classes offered through the university that included parent discussion while the children played in another room. Discipline was a topic that baffled me as a new parent. I was confident about my philosophy on the topic, but what puzzled me was the frustration other parents expressed with their inability to control their children's tantrums, streaks of wild independence, biting, or hitting. I cringed at the very word "discipline" in this context, because it brought to mind images of spanking, berating words, and a mentality reminiscent of old stories about going to bed without supper.

My solution seemed altogether too obvious to me but didn't seem to fit the standard description of child discipline. During one class, the teacher guiding the parent discussion asked me what I did with Ben. I replied, "I believe that if you just sit down with your child, look him in the eye, and talk to him, he'll understand. Ask him what *he* thinks and how *he* feels, and then reason with him from there." Blank expressions hung momentarily on the faces of the other mothers in the discussion circle, and then the teacher said, "That *may* work for Ben...but what about Damien? Sharisa, how do you react when Damien loses control? Tell us about that." And the conversation continued on the same old track it had begun with no further discussion about using Wendy's crazy reasoning strategy that *may* work for Ben, but not for others.

That "crazy" reasoning was a basic strategy I often employed with Ben. I tried to raise his awareness of the situation and teach him to think about a possible solution as we worked together to solve the problem.

I really didn't get it, at the time, that Ben was an exception to the rule of most two-year-olds. Other mothers expressed frustration in their children's repeated impulsive behavior, whether it was hitting a sibling in anger over not getting the toy they wanted or throwing the bowl of Spaghettios on the floor because they wanted macaroni and cheese instead. Ben's actions of anger or rebellion were less physical and more premeditated—as if he put a lot of thought into the most effective method of making his point. If his actions were inappropriate, it usually only took one confrontation and discussion of an alternative more appropriate behavior, and Ben understood. He tried to avoid conflict that would result in displeasing me or his father; it was as if he wanted to be at peace with us. After a short discussion, he usually understood that it was an advantage to him in the long run to choose a more appropriate behavior.

Apparently *I* was an exception to the rule as well. As a parent, I had chosen a different approach than most parents of two-year-olds. My tactic with Ben was more one of logic and reason, guidance and coaching, perhaps more appropriate for a typical five- or six-year-old.

Our Ben was very sensitive to how his actions affected others. He seemed to have developed early his own conscience or self-discipline. Looking back, I can imagine one of those miniature little red devils sitting on his left shoulder and a tiny white angel perched on the other, like in the old cartoons. He must have been making good use of his reasoning skills as he listened to his conscience or his internal thoughts, because he resisted the little devil's talk more and more and took the angel's advice on a daily basis.

Enter Jillian, The Strong Girl

A little sister, Jillian, was born two months short of Ben's third birthday. She was born at 2:37 P.M., after eight hours of labor and nearly the same time of day as her brother. When she came, she entered the world in a flash! Jillian was wide awake, active, and alert from the start. She was not going to be one to lie still and quietly observe like her brother. She soon showed us that she wouldn't be satisfied lingering on the fringes of anything but instead wanted to be in the middle of the action at every moment.

Jillian quickly earned a reputation for being both physically and mentally strong. Although she passed some developmental milestones at similar times as Ben (she sat at five months and walked before 11 months), it was her sheer determination that set her apart, as well as her sense of fearlessness when she explored all avenues of physical activity. By contrast, Ben was usually cautious.

Jillian was socially intense from a young age. One afternoon, in our early childhood family education class, I held a then-seven-month-old Jillian securely in my lap with my left arm while I picked up some toys with my right. Keesha, a six-month-old cherub-like baby, was gently placed on the floor near us nestled in her carrier, maybe six feet to our left, while her mother put her coat away. Suddenly, I felt my weight shift to the left as Jillian began flailing her arms and leaning toward this other baby. Of course, Jillian didn't know that I could have lost hold of her and dropped her from my lap onto the floor. She had only one thing on her mind—to check out Keesha immediately. I dropped the toys and plopped the ever-curious Jillian on the floor next to Keesha. This was a common occurrence. Jillian was determined to get close to the other babies her size or smaller. Whatever the activity, her fascination demanded that her body be in close proximity to the babies, even if it meant falling out of my arms and risking life and limb to get there. She was bent on adventure outdoors as well.

One day in the park, when Jillian was only a year and a half old, I was playing the usual shadow game most parents of adventuresome tots play. I followed Jillian up, down, and across the climbing equipment with my hands hovering at her back as she climbed the stairs of the main tower, then at her ankles as she skittered across the wobbly metal planked bridge to the adjacent twin tower. I was prepared to catch her at the first moment of any misstep on the equipment. Because I was talking to another mother and watching Ben at the same time, my hands and eyes temporarily broke from their synchronized movements. Just then, Jillian took a jerky turn to the right instead of the straight path she'd been traversing, and she decided to take a trip on the big-kid slide instead. Shrieking in alarm as I realized I'd lost sight and touch with her, I dashed toward the end of the wavy yellow slide. I heard a scream and a thud and fully expected to find a frightened, scraped-up little kid in the gravel. Jillian had landed flat on her bottom at the base of the slide and for a moment was frozen in silence. But before I could reach out to pick her up, she jumped to her feet, giggling and laughing, and shouted "Again! I want to go again!"

This was our Jillian. With great physical enthusiasm, "Again!"

Later in the childhood education classes, I found myself heaving a sigh mixed with envy and resignation when other mothers talked about their three- and four-year-old children napping. Napping? Could it be true? Jillian didn't take naps. She'd quit taking them at two. I thought that when Ben returned to nursery school for a second year, I would finally have a break to myself in the afternoons while she napped, but it proved to be wishful thinking. Within weeks of her second birthday, only a month before Ben began nursery school, her body and mind suddenly apparently stopped requiring a nap. Now she wouldn't allow herself to miss anything, *all* day. And I resigned myself to the fact that I now had to wait until she went to kindergarten to get a break. The upside was that if she did take a nap, 100% of the time it was due to an oncoming fever, and I could count on the nap as an accurate diagnostic tool indicating illness. It may interest other parents to know that giving up naps is common with some gifted children.[2]

Compared to Ben, Jillian was not a compliant, agreeable child. She earned the title "Miss Contrary," as in the nursery rhyme "Mary, Mary Quite Contrary," and she and I had many laughs over the concept of contrariness when she was just two and three years old (and we still do). On one particularly trying day, I said, more to myself than to Jillian, "Whew, I am dead tired after chasing you around the house all day." Jillian turned toward me and quickly proclaimed, "No you're not, Mom. You're not dead." I stretched my arms out in a zombie-like pose and teased her, "Oh, yes I am, Miss Contrary. Aaargh. I am the walking dead mother, too tired to chase after Miss Contrary—until now!" Jillian took off running down the hall with a screech, hysterically laughing all the way as I plodded after her.

Jillian was strong-willed and definitely had a mind of her own. After one challenging day, I explained the predicament to my husband, "I'm *so* tired of her objections to everything! I'm okay if her objections are negotiable within the situation, but if I were to give in, even just once, when it's *not* okay—I mean, sometimes I think it would just be easier to give it up with her. But if I did, she'd be horrible! But on the other hand…." I was trying to work this out for myself. "…if I were totally overbearing, that might be worse, and we'd be in a power struggle. I worry that if she doesn't have the chance to at least express herself, she might stuff it all inside and explode. Or worse yet, maybe she would simply wither up."

In time, I discovered that what Jillian most needed was some room for self-expression and the freedom to make some of her own decisions and to determine her own direction. Certainly, she needed strong, firm guidance, but she also needed a certain amount of flexibility and sensitivity from someone who believed in her and encouraged her strength and energy as assets.

We offered Jillian choices whenever we could so that she could assert her sense of control. She could choose her own clothes to wear for the day; choose between colored pencils, crayons, or markers; or help plan the menu for dinner with what choice of fruit she wanted. If she came up with her own idea of an option, I would weigh it carefully, and if it was more beneficial than not, I would encourage her to follow through with it. I was also sure to give her a "high five" or a smile of agreement to show her when I appreciated her inventive solution. If she came up with a choice that was not within reason, I tried to craft a revised version, emphasize its strong points, and then propose the new alternative. For example, if she insisted on buying Twinkies at the grocery store for the third time in a row, I would offer a new selection of alternative choices, "Instead of Twinkies, how about graham crackers, ginger snaps, or fruit snacks? You know, graham crackers and ginger snaps are good for dunking in a glass of milk too." If she was determined on getting the Twinkies, which would be typical about 50% of the time, I would resort to Plan B: "Since we've already bought Twinkies on the last two shopping trips, it's not a choice this time. You need a little variety. You can either choose from these three options or nothing at all. You decide." Swiftly explaining my position with a logical reason for it and standing my ground was accompanied by the continued forward motion of the shopping cart. More groceries needed to be bought, and I wouldn't make a big deal about our disagreement. Usually by the time we got to the other end of the isle, Jillian would have proclaimed her decision, and I'd let her run back and retrieve her choice.

Jillian was passionate about life, and she let you know it. Besides her physical precociousness, she was in high gear emotionally and socially. She could be in tears of frustration one instant because her shoe didn't get onto her foot satisfactorily, and the next moment howling in laughter at her own joke about how she could now walk like a dog with a broken foot. She showed just as little fear of climbing a tall slide and speeding down as she would in meeting a new friend in the grocery store checkout line. "Cautious" and "shy" were not words in this Strong Girl's vocabulary.

Both of our children were very bright and precocious—we were later to learn they were highly or exceptionally gifted—but their personalities were very different. They both had different ways of presenting their "self" to the world.

Chapter 2

I Want My Mommy!

When Jillian was a baby, Ben went to nursery school three mornings a week. That first year, our sensitive Ben had acute separation anxiety. Every morning, emotional and physical battles inevitably ended in tears and pleas for me not to leave the school. The nursery school teacher tried to distract him as best she could, but she often had to physically hold him back when I walked out the door. She said that he showed more determination than most other kids to keep me in sight and engaged. I made sure to have an ample supply of Kleenex in the car.

My spies—teachers and friends who dropped their children off after I did—reported that Ben stopped crying almost as soon as I left. They said that when I walked out of the building, he retreated to the quieter dress-up and science area and hid under a table for a while. From beneath the table filled with bones, pine cones, and sea shells—all nature objects children had brought from home—Ben would refuse the offers made by the teacher to join the group. The teacher casually but purposely invited him out, encouraging him gently and yet firmly. But no amount of persuasion could convince Ben to join the other children until he was ready to do it on his own. He sometimes waited as long as 30 minutes, until he was absolutely sure that the teachers and other children were no longer a threat. Or perhaps he waited until he had thoroughly checked out the situation to decide if he wanted to participate. Then, under his own power, he would emerge and proceed to play and interact comfortably the rest of the morning until I picked him up with happy hugs and smiles.

As the year progressed, I realized that Ben had transformed his original innocent separation anxiety into "Mommy-manipulation." His self-imposed isolation under the table shortened in duration, and before long, he didn't bother hiding anymore. Once I learned that he didn't seem to mind our separation after the door closed and I was out of sight, I adjusted accordingly and stopped feeling sorry for the little guy. His game was up. With my new understanding of the situation, I decided that I would show no pity whatsoever and speak very little of the separation issue so as not to draw more attention to it. When the subject came up, I spoke with confidence that Ben was handling school just fine. By the end of that first year, he could say good-bye bravely and contentedly. He learned to trust his surroundings, the teacher, and some other children in the group. More importantly, he learned to trust in himself and his newfound independence.

Nursery school was a place primarily for Ben to test and build his social skills. The philosophy of the school was not one of rote academic emphasis, but rather more of providing the opportunity for the children to learn to trust others, develop friendships, and practice fine and gross motor skills activities with a sampling of very basic academics. They had a broad variety of activity choices that changed from week to week. The first hour was devoted to activities of each child's choosing; they played dress-up, pretend house, puzzles, beading, Playmobile, and Play Doh. They could try new things or choose an activity that provided a secure comfort level and appropriate stimulation. Most often, Ben chose to interact with one other boy in imaginative quiet play with the puzzles, Playmobile, or the large wooden building blocks. He never chose the dress-up area, nor did he like the idea of carousing around in the large motor area on the tricycles, jump ropes, or large rubber balls. He enjoyed these large motor activities at home, but he chose not to do them in a crowd of other children during that first year at school.

Ben was very selective when choosing friends. There was a large core group of boisterous boys who played loudly and exclusively in the large muscle area. He was friendly with the boisterous boys, but he had no interest in their wild play. Instead, he chose to play with one friend in their own fantasy play world of castles and knights or alien space travel.

By January of that first year of nursery school, Ben, now three years old, displayed a growing interest in the math concepts of addition, multiplication, calendars, and time. One day, while we were in the car backing out of the driveway, Ben watched the paneled automatic garage door close in front of us and asked, "Mom, is four times eight 32?" I stopped the van, turned around, and faced him as he sat buckled in his car seat next to Jillian. "Yes...," I said, studying his face. Where had that come from? What was he thinking? As if to answer my silent question, Ben continued, "The garage door has four rows of those squares, and each row has eight squares." He hunched his shoulders slightly. "I was just curious."

At about this same time, Ben got his first digital wrist watch, and the two were inseparable. We'd joke about what color his skin had become underneath the wrist band when he insisted on keeping it on during his bath. The watch was waterproof, so what would the point be if he *didn't* wear it in the bathtub? Through experimentation, he quickly figured out how to set the time, date, stopwatch, and alarm. If we were late in picking him up from a friend's house, he would tell us down to the exact second how late we were. If he was anticipating watching NOVA, a favorite television show, he would give us the countdown until its broadcast. He and his father would periodically synchronize their watches and debate whose was more accurate according to atomic time.

I wondered if another year of nursery school would be beneficial for him or if an early kindergarten entrance might be better. I worried that he would be bored with another year of nursery school. I thought kindergarten might be the best next step, especially since he had an October birthday.

Decisions like this are usually influenced by a school district's calendar. Nursery school registration in our district was in January and February for the following September—a full eight to nine months into the future! I had to base my decision on what I knew right then and there, even if the situation drastically changed between January and September. I was uneasy about making a commitment so far in advance.

A month earlier, when I had commented to my mother about Ben's experiences at nursery school, she'd said, "You're going to send Ben to kindergarten early, aren't you?" It was more of an assumption than a true question. At that time, I hadn't thought of it quite so bluntly. In fact, I hadn't really thought about kindergarten at all. Ben had just started nursery school; after all, he was only three years old, and I wasn't mentally ready to think about kindergarten yet.

My mother's certainty came from 10 years of involvement with the Minnesota Council for Gifted and Talented (MCGT), where she held numerous positions ranging from president to newsletter editor to front lines phone counselor. She had raised five very bright children of her own and had a master's degree in gifted education. She obviously knew and cared about gifted children and their families. However, she kept a respectful distance, knowing that I knew Ben best. As for me, I had my doubts about my ability to make the best choices for Ben. He was academically more than ready for kindergarten, but was he socially ready?

I began asking people—anyone—what they thought about Ben going to kindergarten early. His nursery school teacher was solidly in favor of him staying in nursery school another year. "He has plenty of time, and childhood is rushed enough as it is," she said. "I would give him another year to himself, to just be a kid, before sending him to kindergarten."

My oldest sister told me about her daughter, Breanna, and how she compared with another classmate who entered kindergarten early. "Breanna is one of the oldest in the class, and she's developed great leadership skills. But I know another mother whose daughter, Kelsey, is the youngest in her class because she went to kindergarten a year early." The expression on my sister's face turned to furrowed eyebrows and deep concern. "That mother regrets having rushed her child. Because she's the youngest, she struggles. She's not in the lead academically in her class like she used to be, and her self-esteem has taken a beating because of it. I'd much rather give a child a chance to be a leader with age on her side than have to struggle and feel like she's not fitting in with her classmates."

I asked other people as well, although none of them were professionals. Other than my mother, no one else spoke very positively about early entrance. In the end, the advice from Ben's nursery school teacher and my sister influenced me the most. It seemed the safest decision with the least amount of risk. We decided to keep Ben in nursery school one more year.

Superman Saves the Day

That second year of nursery school turned out to be one of utmost excitement for Ben. Instead of going in the mornings, he attended the afternoon session, with fewer children and less chaos. Then, too, he was a year older with a little experience under his belt. The separation anxiety resurfaced briefly for just a week or two, and then he was on his way. Instead of avoiding the mainstream, he created his own stream!

For Christmas, Ben and Jillian each received a blue Superman shirt from their grandmother. Before the first day of returning to nursery school after winter break, Ben asked if I would pin his red Superman cape from his old pajamas onto his new Superman shirt so he could wear it to school. That cape and blue shirt with the big yellow S on the front became his self-imposed nursery school uniform. He insisted on wearing it every day. The cape request was followed by a request to make a police badge. So I cut out a badge shape from cardboard, wrapped it in aluminum foil, wrote *Captain Ben* on it in permanent marker, and sealed it with clear packing tape. All that next week, Ben wore his badge pinned to the front of his Superman shirt. Soon he requested badges for the other children, and tickets and police notebooks with pencils. He built a loyal following in nursery school. Every day, with three other boys and one girl as his fellow officers, he wrote tickets for speeding teachers and caught burglar children in the playhouse area.

Kindergarten Anxiety

During Ben's second year of nursery school, kindergarten was in the front of my mind. When I was a child, kindergarten was never an issue. There was no kindergarten. You either went to public school for first grade like most of the other kids, or if you were Catholic, you went to parochial school at St. Peter's. I felt overwhelmed with the many possibilities available to us— public school, home school, traditional private school, parochial school, and more recently, a new experimental Spanish immersion school offered through our public school district.

I did some research into these options. Parochial school was out because our family was not religiously inclined. Home school was not an option philosophically at that time because I firmly believed in mainstream public school education. (Now, in hindsight, if I could do it again, I would consider home schooling along with the other options.) The problem was that I couldn't imagine Ben in a regular public school because I feared that he would be bored in that setting. My only two remaining options, then, were the enticing choices of traditional private school or the new Spanish immersion school.

I called three of the most prestigious and well-known private schools in our area and requested that information be sent to our home. Glossy brochures arrived within the week. The private schools had several characteristics in common: they prided themselves in providing top quality education; they emphasized, both verbally and visually, that the schools were not exclusively for white upper-class families; and they were all prohibitively expensive.

I knew that there was no way we could afford private school tuition for any of these schools. The only way it seemed remotely possible for Ben to attend would be for us to win the lottery. I decided to stop looking further at the private schools. In a way, this was a cop-out because I didn't have to make a decision or even visit the schools. I wrote it off based solely on our inability to pay.

Perhaps more importantly, however, my decision was reinforced by an impression that a private school might not meet Ben's needs for a more advanced curriculum. Ben was a kid who had a way of thinking and behaving that was way beyond the expected grade level. When I spoke to one private school admissions office by phone, I was startled by the pompous response I received after briefly explaining Ben's situation. "*All* of our students are gifted," the admissions representative said, with emphasis on the word "all." Reading between the lines, it was clear to me that she assumed, sight unseen, that my son was no different than any of the other children they admitted. How could she know? She didn't bother to inquire for details, and I wasn't about to offer them freely after the tone of voice she used in her proclamation.

I later read in the school's application packet that they would only consider children who scored 115 or higher on an intelligence test. I disagreed with the assumption that gifted meant the same as above average. And besides, Ben didn't seem simply above average. He was way out there somewhere else. He was *really* different from most kids his age. I considered the attitude of the admissions representative and the limited number of students and teachers at the private school. How could I expect a private school to provide the flexibility and range of opportunities that Ben would need? Put off by my first brief and uncomfortable personal contact with the school, I didn't pursue it further. Looking back now, I realize that I didn't give *any* of the private schools a fair shake by making personal visits to the campuses and classrooms. I went by my first impression.

All along, I had a special fondness for the new Spanish immersion school in our local district. Because I had been an exchange student to South America my year after high school, I knew and appreciated first hand the benefits of language and cultural immersion. I thought this school might be a good choice for Ben.

When Ben started his second year of nursery school, the Spanish immersion school was just starting its first year with three kindergarten classes. Each subsequent year, the school would add one more grade until it became a full K-6 school.

I visited one of the new kindergarten classes during school hours. The classroom was bursting with bright, colorful paper creations made by the children. Spanish words were posted everywhere, identifying time, numbers, colors, animals, and common objects. Every bit of space except for the large carpeted center of the room was filled. There were interesting learning centers for science, fantasy play, a puppet theater, and a cozy reading corner. Señor Lempke, the teacher, was tall and young-looking, which belied the fact that he had several years of teaching experience under his belt. His teaching style radiated enthusiasm, and I could see his energy and love of the Spanish language and learning reflected in the children's eyes. The children sat in a circle singing a Spanish naming game. One by one, to the rhythm of the music, each child dared to speak the new Spanish words with giggles and clapping. My fear of possible boredom for Ben melted away as I observed this amazing scene.

Brown and Gray Kindergarten

So in the fall of the following year, when he was four but would soon be five, Ben began kindergarten at the Spanish immersion school. Less than a week later, he came home from school one day and pronounced in a melancholy, desperate tone of voice, "Mom, I'm bored."

Ben's confession did not come as a surprise. Doubts about his situation had begun to creep into the back of my mind when we found out that he was placed in the new teacher's class instead of Señor Lempke's. I was disappointed but still optimistic that Señora Viera would be just fine. She was an experienced teacher who had taught in the district previously.

I convinced myself of this in spite of a meeting with Señora Viera a few days before school began. The classroom had a high ceiling but otherwise was cramped and drab. There were no identifying characteristics that led me to believe that active, imaginative, energetic kindergartners would want to spend their days in such a room. Stacks of half-emptied boxes were haphazardly stacked on top of tables and on the floor, and the high walls were bare. The room left me with a sense of browns and grays. As a person, Señora Viera struck me as neither especially vibrant nor especially inept. She was as dull and non-committal as the room.

Still, I remained positive about the school. I convinced myself that Señora Viera was new and was still getting organized. By the time school started, I thought, this room will be buzzing with joyful children and activity. Once the year began, however, the room didn't change. I saw no evidence of joyfully buzzing activity among the other children. When I picked Ben up one day, I asked him, "What did you do during your free time today?"

He said, with no enthusiasm, "If we finish or have free time, we can only do puzzles or look at books." When I asked him the same question a week later, his response was nearly identical, except this time, he punctuated it with a heavy dismal sigh. The children were limited to only two choices during free time every single day, just as he said: puzzles or books. No imaginary play, puppet play, Lego building, crafts, science exploration, or musical instruments. No wonder he was bored.

I am ashamed to say that most of the rest of Ben's kindergarten year is a hazy blur in my memory. I continued to persist in my hopes that things would improve—that he would latch onto Spanish, connect with his teacher and classmates, and begin to truly enjoy kindergarten. I continued to give his teacher the benefit of the doubt and excused her lack of enthusiasm and inability to inspire her students as a result of inexperience in teaching in a language immersion environment. I persisted in telling myself that things would get better, that she just needed more time.

There were two significant events that I do recall that took place early in the school year after Ben's confession of boredom. I spoke to Señora Viera about Ben's complaint, and somewhere in our brief discussion, I mentioned to her that he loved comic books. Soon afterward, she produced several Spanish comic books for Ben to read during free time. After that simple and genuine gesture, Ben seemed a little more connected with Señora Viera.

The second event took place while I was volunteering one morning in Ben's classroom. The children had a worksheet that showed a dozen monkeys climbing in a large tree, each holding a different shape. The children were instructed in Spanish to color each shape a certain color: red for circles, yellow for triangles, and blue for the squares. As I made my way around the tables, I noticed that most of the children were half finished, while Ben's paper had only two shapes colored correctly but sloppily. It appeared that Ben was having trouble following directions or making the connection between each shape and color. I knew that he had learned to identify his shapes and colors as a toddler and that he was more than capable of following these directions, even in Spanish. I asked him if he understood and encouraged him to continue, but I could see from the hastily scribbled red and blue shapes and the abandoned crayons lying in front of him on the table that he had no intention of participating further in the activity. He leaned back limply in his chair and watched the other children with a blank expression on his face. I could imagine his little mind saying to himself, "What's the point?" To others, this may have been an exercise in language, color, and shape identification. But Ben saw things differently. It was his first introduction to busywork.

How could I have let this situation persist for an entire year? I think my eternal optimism and naiveté as an inexperienced parent played major roles. There may have been some denial in there, too. I convinced myself that it "wasn't too bad" because kindergarten was only for the morning, and he still had the whole rest of the day to spend in self-directed adventures with Jillian and me at home. I wholeheartedly believed in the philosophy of the Spanish immersion program as well, and I hoped that once Ben adopted more Spanish, school would become more interesting and the world would open up for him in a way that traditional public school could not offer.

I also held out hope for first grade and a new teacher, full-day classes, and most of all, having some gifted and talented services for Ben. The school district tested kindergartners who were recommended by their teachers and/or parents for the gifted and talented program. The children were given *The Cognitive Abilities Test* in small groups. Then, based on how well they scored and with teacher observations and other input, approximately 5% of kindergartners across the district qualified for gifted and talented services in first grade. I made sure that Señora Viera recommended Ben for the testing that spring.

Ben took the test in April without much fanfare, and later we received a letter in the mail with a test score sheet. The letter explained that Ben qualified for gifted services, that his scores were on the accompanying sheet, and that we would be contacted in the fall about the gifted program. We were relieved to hear that Ben would be in the gifted program—whatever it would entail—and we looked forward to hearing from the gifted and talented teacher in the fall.

Uno, Dos, Tres

Fall arrived, and with it our hopes that the new school year would offer Ben a more challenging curriculum. His first-grade teacher was energetic, professional, and had a general handle on authority—all characteristics that were sorely lacking in Ben's kindergarten teacher.

Señora Cruz was a petite, young, and intelligent woman with black shining hair and large dark eyes. Spanish was her native language; she was born and raised in Mexico to parents who put a high priority on education. Her mother was a teacher for many years and had inspired her daughter to become one as well. Her spoken English was a little rough, but she was still an effective communicator. Colorful posters and pictures decorated her classroom walls. There were bold words that one would expect in any first-grade classroom, except that instead of one, two, three…the words said uno, dos, tres.…*Everything* was in Spanish.

That first week went by without any major complaints from Ben. He quickly adjusted to the new teacher, new classmates, and new schedule. I am not sure what our exact expectations were except that we hoped he would find more stimulation and less busywork in this new class.

After a few weeks of the usual notes and announcements, my heart dropped to my stomach when the first of several math homework sheets came home accompanied by explanation sheets to the parents. The worksheets that came home in Ben's backpack were full of exercises in tallying; counting by ones, twos, fives, and tens; and observing how numbers are used at home on the oven, clock, thermometer, etc. I cringed at the sight of these homework sheets because they addressed concepts that Ben had discovered on his own two and even three years earlier. When Ben began questioning me, asking, "Why do I have to do this?" I couldn't give him a reasonable explanation except that, for most of the kids in his class, these were concepts they likely hadn't encountered before and the teacher intended for them to learn something useful. So why did Ben have to do these simple sheets? Because the teacher said so. Welcome to classroom politics.

My husband and I had many nights of discussions about the inappropriateness of what Ben was being asked to do in class. We decided that mathematics was the most concrete subject about which we could approach his teacher. There could be no denying Ben's advanced abilities in math and his need for more appropriate math studies.

Although math was as natural to Ben as breathing and playing, he was no slouch at reading either. When he was three, he was displaying sure signs of being on the edge of cracking the English linguistic code. Fascinated by the Garfield and Calvin and Hobbes books, he would take them along with him in the car on our errands. While I drove down the street, I could hear his voice from the back seat as he sounded out and figured out words. One afternoon on the way to nursery school, he chuckled aloud to himself and said, "Mom! Look. This is Ka-POW!" and in his excitement, he thrust the comic book into my face. The sound effects exploding from the humorous drawings impressed him most. I was sure he was on the verge of reading independently.

In kindergarten, he showed no signs of further reading progress, however. By the time he was in first grade, I began to worry in earnest. He developed a rote memory of 40 to 60 Spanish sight words and numerous English words, and he understood much of the Spanish spoken in class, but he could not read any better than he did when he was three. His teacher told me, "He's right on track for a first grader."

Señora Cruz didn't understand my concerns with Ben's average performance. Why would a parent be dissatisfied with an average performance? My dissatisfaction involved more than a perceived average performance. Several points factored into my concern. I knew that in this case, average performance was a misfit for this "non-average" child. Ben had begun reading on his own before kindergarten, but he had made little progress since that time. And since he was a highly verbal kid, I thought he should have a naturally higher interest in reading—at least the same interest that he expressed when he was a preschooler. More recently, and of even greater concern, his behavior had changed. Ben was not his usual happy-go-lucky self.

If Ben had been happy in the school environment and with his accomplishments thus far, I wouldn't have worried. But in spite of his average, "to be expected" performance in reading and writing, he was angrily resisting independent reading in either language—as if he were being forced to eat a pickled herring. Perhaps it was a motivation issue. Perhaps the frustration of everything else at school was spilling over into reading.

I began sitting with Ben on his bed every night and working with him on his English reading. He had a low tolerance for mistakes and was easily frustrated, but I encouraged him to keep trying. I read to him and Jillian on a daily basis, and I wondered if this was actually to his disadvantage. Perhaps he would never feel the need to read by himself because I was always there to read to him.

His disdain for reading and for communication in Spanish troubled me. He had never shown a negative attitude toward learning before. My hopes for him developing a love for the Spanish language faded with each frustrating day. However, I learned later that there was more to his frustration than simply the language immersion environment.

At the end of every school day, I waited for Ben on the front lawn of our house. The bus dropped him off at our curb, and he and I would greet each other with hugs and kisses. "Hi! How was your day?" I would ask, and Ben usually responded with, "Great! What's for snack?" Three-year-old Jillian waited excitedly with me. She missed him during the day and looked forward to playing with him when he got home.

By the end of September, Ben's character had changed during this daily ritual. He jumped off that last step of the bus a little more slowly, and his little body appeared weighted down by an extra 10 pounds in his backpack. We all still hugged and kissed, but on one particular day as we walked toward the house, I noticed a big change in Ben. He seemed like a different child.

Whereas he usually greeted Jillian with encouragement and a touch of big brotherly care, on this day, as she tried to see what surprises he had brought home in his backpack, he suddenly snapped. "Leave my things alone!" he yelled and shoved her aside. She froze and quickly withdrew her hand from Ben's backpack, tears welling in her eyes and her breath quickening.

I gently guided Ben into the house. Within moments, he and I were alone in my bedroom with the door closed. "Ben," I began, "Jillian wasn't trying to bother you on purpose. She's just interested in you and cares about you, and what you said and did are *not* okay. I don't understand why you acted that way. That's just not like you. What's going on?"

Ben's eyes welled up with tears, and a remorseful, "I'm sorry," whispered from his lips as he hugged me tightly, sobbing into my shoulder.

A nagging streak of anger crept into Ben's every action that week. I had never seen him act out this way. Something was definitely not right in his life. Since nothing had changed at home, the only logical thing was that something was going on at school. Ben and I talked about school, but he couldn't really put his finger on anything in particular. He couldn't explain why he was so grouchy. He seemed as puzzled as I.

Little Chairs, Little Meetings

Brian and I met with Ben's teacher during the last week of September, hoping to find some answers to help us understand Ben's unhappiness at school and how we might help. Señora Cruz was sympathetic to the situation. She emphasized that adjusting to all-day school, and particularly in the Spanish environment, could be a difficult and a highly stressful thing for some kids. She said that Ben seemed happy in school and that he was by no means a troublemaker. In fact, he was always very obedient and respectful of the rules and of others. "Let's give him a few more weeks," she said. "The first month of first grade is a huge adjustment while we work on setting a routine and on classroom relationships."

We thought our first contact with Señora Cruz was fairly positive. On her advice, we decided we would just relax and give Ben some room and some more time. We could wait and see how he was in a few weeks.

The wait-and-see plan lasted about five days. By the first week of October, it was painfully clear to me that Ben was experiencing more than the typical difficulty in adapting to first-grade life. If I had paid closer attention to our previous conversation with Señora Cruz, I might have read between the lines: "we work on setting a *routine* and on classroom relationships" translated into tedious frustration for Ben. He was eager to start learning, really digging into the wonderful world of knowledge. Kindergarten was for little kids. Now that he had that out of the way, he was ready for the really serious stuff. Ben made a comment one day that seemed to reflect his now clarified feelings. "Mom, I love to learn, and I'm not *learning* anything." He complied with all of the classroom rules and procedures and rituals, but his patience was running out very quickly with every tally mark counted, every color identified, and every alphabet song sung.

Beginning in October, while volunteering in the classroom, I could observe the other students while reading books to the children and helping with special projects. It struck me how different all the other children were from Ben, especially the boys. Rough play and language were typical of the boys in his classroom. They were not necessarily naughty, but they had a different code of behavior, which seemed to put Ben in an awkward and uncomfortable position. It reminded me of his first year of preschool. Ben didn't seem to even want to socialize with these boys. He was very comfortable doing things by himself, and he simply wasn't interested in mimicking macho behavior like they were. He was different. He was more sensitive. He used considerate language at all times and enjoyed friendships with the girls just as much as with the boys. Some of his discomfort seemed to stem from a resistance to conform to what appeared to be the social norm for boys in the first grade.[3]

In kindergarten, Ben became friends with a girl named Heidi. She was tall, strong, and talkative, and yet she retained a baby-like innocence. Like Ben, she was the oldest child in the family, with two younger brothers. Now Heidi was in first grade with Ben—one of only two children he knew from kindergarten. She and Ben often played together.

Heidi wasn't afraid to show how she felt about most anything, and it didn't take long once first grade began for Ben to realize that she also wanted his undivided attention. Besides the frustrations of not reading, not being challenged in math, and not wanting to play macho-type games with the other boys, Ben now had to deal with Heidi's overwhelming affection for him. She wanted to sit at the table with him, sit on the carpet beside him, stand in line next to him, eat lunch with him, play on the playground with him, and be with him everywhere all the time. She began to call and invite him to play after school. Ben liked her, but he was quickly losing his desire to play with her all the time.

We began to realize that our bright but sensitive little guy was experiencing so many pressures during the school day— speaking, reading, listening to Spanish, doing math work that he'd been capable of doing since age three, trying to fit in with the boys without acting outside of his own personal code of conduct—and now he was having to deal with Heidi's constant displays of pressing affection. He felt trapped. Maybe he was suffocating.

During the second week of October, just days before the school's official fall conferences, Brian and I requested another meeting with Ben's teacher. We had discussed our previous conference for many nights and decided that we would try to tackle what we perceived to be the easiest battle first—the battle we thought we could most easily win—and that was Ben's math curriculum. We came to this noon-hour meeting with the specific goal of getting Ben into a higher level math group. If we could just improve that one subject for Ben, the subject he most loved, then, we thought, the rest of school might be more bearable while we "just gave him some time to adjust, to see how he does."

The meeting involved so much discussion with his teacher that we decided to schedule yet another meeting, this time to include Mrs. Jansen, the gifted and talented teacher for the district's K-3 students. Were we making progress? We weren't sure. In our own indirect way, perhaps. At least we were talking with the school staff about our serious concerns. Señora Cruz promised us that she would try to work something out for Ben, but she would first seek some guidance from Mrs. Jansen. However, when we asked about accelerating Ben to second grade for math, she said that it would be impossible because of the language barrier. "Ben needs to develop the language. If he goes for math with the second graders, he will be placed with students who have nearly three times the exposure to Spanish than he. He really must have the language and the vocabulary first."

Shortly after this meeting, we met with Señora Cruz and Ben for the official fall conference on goal-setting. The week before, Ben had brought home a goal sheet with the assignment to write two goals for himself for the year—one social and one academic. Ben's social goal for himself was to simply make more friends. His academic goal was to learn division by the end of the year. (Division is traditionally introduced in the fourth grade.) His goal sheet also contained a section for parents to complete. We agreed with Ben's goals to build friendships at school and to have the opportunity to be part of a more challenging math group. The official fall conference was brief, and our goals—both ours and Ben's—were noted for the record.

First-Grade Turning Point

Now, at our fourth conference, I thought that I should have been accustomed to sitting in the tiny blue plastic chairs at the squatty round worktable in Señora Cruz's room. Brian and I arrived five minutes early. As we waited for the gifted teacher to arrive, I came to the conclusion that I was just too large, too wide, and too tall. I had outgrown this little chair some 30-odd years ago, and yet I had to make do with it because there were no other chairs. There were no other choices in this room. This must be what it's like for Ben, I thought, as I adjusted my legs for the third time in three minutes. There were no other choices in the class for him, even though he'd long ago outgrown the activities. But instead of putting up with cramped legs for a half-hour meeting, he had to put up with a cramped brain every hour of every school day.

My thoughts were interrupted when Mrs. Jansen entered the room, and Señora Cruz introduced us. The four of us sat around the table, and I began with our concerns for Ben and his math curriculum. Brian and I emphasized that Ben's lack of challenge was not limited to mathematics, but that math seemed to be the clearest issue to address at present. Then Brian let me do most of the talking. I again asked if we could put Ben with other kids for a higher-level math group, or if he could move up to second grade for math—just for that one subject.

Mrs. Jansen graciously acknowledged our concerns and then proceeded to enlighten us as to what the second graders in her gifted and talented group had completed thus far in her pullout program. "This is just to give you an idea of where the second graders are," she said as she laid out several sheets with colorful diagrams elaborately and meticulously drawn and labeled in children's handwriting. "I brought a few examples of projects from our fall unit on the brain for you to see." The finely executed anatomical reference sheets felt intimidating. Ben was nowhere close to such examples of perfection on paper. But I failed to see the connection between these brain diagrams and Ben's ability to do multiplication. I began to wonder if Mrs. Jansen understood or was even listening to our concerns about the situation at hand.

"Wow, these are great…but as far as Ben goes," I prodded the conversation back on track, "is there some way we could determine where exactly his abilities and achievement are in math? I believe he can easily work on a second-grade level in math, but I have no idea what the second-grade math objectives are or how he compares to those objectives."

After some roundabout discussion, Mrs. Jansen expressed support of Señora Cruz's position that Ben's lack of experience with the Spanish language would make it impossible for him to move up to second-grade math.

I then pursued the idea of special grouping in his grade for math.

I wasn't prepared for Mrs. Jansen's response. She told us that ability grouping was impossible because Ben's test scores on the *Cognitive Ability Test* were so unlike those of his age peers that there was simply no one to group him with. Mrs. Jansen explained to us that there were no other first graders in the school who came close to matching his computational cognitive ability. Of all the kindergartners in the entire district who were tested the year before, Ben had scored by far the highest. I was not surprised that he did well, but I *was* surprised that no one else had even come close. Was he that different from other kids his age?

This revelation was followed by the first proactive suggestion. Mrs. Jansen said she couldn't promise, but she suggested that perhaps Mary Vanasek, the Gifted and Talented Education Coordinator and teacher at one of the intermediate schools, could spend a half hour with Ben once a week over several weeks to evaluate his math abilities. Mrs. Vanasek could then report back to Mrs. Jansen, and we all could meet again before the winter break to discuss where to go from there.

"That would give me more time to get to know Ben, too," Señora Cruz added. "And in the meantime, I can talk with Mrs. Jansen about what I can do for Ben in giving him more challenging math work. Then, if Mrs. Vanasek can see Ben for a few weeks, we can wait and see what she finds out and go from there."

Brian and I left the conference thanking everyone for their time. I turned to Mrs. Jansen and said, "Please do call Mrs. Vanasek and let me know if she can meet with Ben." Not fully satisfied with the outcome of this meeting, I concluded as we shook hands, "We'll still have to think about this, and I'll get back to you, Señora Cruz."

It seemed like a fine idea. At least Ben could demonstrate one-on-one what he was capable of doing. But it would mean once again putting off any kind of actual decision or action plan until the third week of December. I was beginning to think that the secret purpose of parent-teacher conferences was to just delay things and schedule more conferences.

I was confident that both Mrs. Jansen and Señora Cruz wanted to help Ben and that they were willing to pursue the limited options available to them to provide him with the appropriate challenges within the confines of the school. However, there was no denying that the second language was a major issue and that time was against Ben. He couldn't wait to acquire the language skills first; he needed to move forward in math *now.* I consider myself a very patient person, sometimes to a fault. But in this instance, I could not justify any more patience at Ben's expense. I was being asked to wait again for another month and a half to reassess his situation, yet I felt an enormous sense of urgency to implement an immediate change to improve Ben's daily learning activities.

His emotional health was at stake. I worried that if his classroom situation remained static, Ben would continue to display anger and a sense of exasperation and helplessness. Waiting even another week, let alone six weeks, to experience positive change in his activities was an eternity to his seven-year-old mind. Each day his emotional situation was slipping downhill, and I felt that the longer it persisted, the longer and harder it would be for him to climb back up.

The End of Wait and See

"Wait and see, wait and see! How long do we have to wait and see before this kid is pummeled to the ground by the invisible hands of boredom and frustration?" I found myself muttering as we climbed into our car to drive home. After the kids had gone to bed, Brian and I had a lengthy discussion about the day's meeting.

"How long do we wait? We've been proactive. We've communicated with the staff," I said. "I just don't think it's possible for Señora Cruz to really get to know Ben in a group of 24 other kids in only a couple of months, and I don't want to wait any longer. Ben's unhappy. Even if Señora Cruz were to give him different work to do, she still doesn't have any idea what he's capable of doing. She said Ben is the first gifted student she's ever had. She's so willing, Brian, but I don't want Ben to be a guinea pig any more than he has to."

"What are our options?" Brian's voice rose. "Why can't the school just test him and resolve some of the mystery of what Ben needs? Wouldn't it help at least to make a plan for him?"

"They did test him in kindergarten, but I'm not sure it showed specifics of what he can actually do or if it compared his ability to kids in other grades. They don't give kids math tests or intelligence tests or whatever tests unless a child is diagnosed as having learning problems..." I caught my breath. "There's no money for the school system to test Ben with a more complete and accurate test unless he falls into the Special Education category at the other end," I ended with a heavy sigh.

We were silent for a few seconds when it suddenly dawned on me. "Who's to say *we* can't have Ben tested? I mean, why wait around for the school? We could get Ben tested privately, and then we'd really know what we're dealing with. It could take the entire school year for Señora Cruz to get to know Ben. Why bang our heads against the wall any longer if we can do something about it now?"

Brian echoed my thoughts, "And we'd know what we're talking about, too. No one could say it's just our opinion or that we're pushing Ben." Why hadn't we thought of this before? We expected the school to be more aware of Ben's needs and to be more flexible in meeting those needs. Well, we would do our best to discover his actual ability and achievement level.

The next morning, I called around and got a referral for a reputable, experienced psychologist who specialized in testing gifted children. I phoned him, explained our predicament, and made an appointment for the coming weekend, just three days after Ben's seventh birthday.

Chapter 3

When the Saints Go Marching In

Ben and I opted for the carpeted stairs rather than taking the elevator to the fourth floor of the small office building. The day was young, and the low sun streaming through the windows of the stairwell warmed our faces at every floor. When we got to the fourth floor, Ben couldn't resist looking out the floor-to-ceiling-window at all the traffic down below. We both admired the city water tower, a familiar local landmark in the distance. In my right hand was the questionnaire that Brian and I had completed the night before, and in my left, I held Ben's small, warm hand.

We found room number 420 and entered a modest reception area where Dr. Mullen greeted us with handshakes. He was Dustin Hoffman incarnate, but since Dustin Hoffman was still alive, Dr. Mullen would pass for his brother. He led us into a larger, windowless office where the testing would take place. I handed Dr. Mullen the parent questionnaire. He thanked me and invited us to sit down while he gave Ben and me a basic rundown of the testing routine.

"Ben, your mom will wait for us just outside the door while you and I go through several activities." Ben listened to Dr. Mullen and nodded in a self-assured attentive posture as his legs dangled from the chair. "We'll see how many questions you can answer and what kind of ideas you have." Turning to me, Dr.

Mullen explained in brief detail what the tests (the *Stanford-Binet Intelligence Scale* and the *Woodcock-Johnson Tests of Achievement*) were and about how long each one would take. Then he spoke to Ben again. "The tests I'm going to give you will help us to see how smart you are and how much you already know how to do. Do you have any questions before we start, Ben? Wendy?" We both shook our heads to indicate no. "Very well. Wendy, we'll see you when we take a break in about an hour and a half."

I closed the door behind me and sat on the brown vinyl sofa outside the inner office. For the next hour or so, I read a book. Since it was Saturday, the entire building was eerily quiet, and I was content to fill my head with my own thoughts. More than once, I discreetly put my ear up to the wooden veneer door of the inner office, but alas, I was unsuccessful in detecting anything audible from the other side.

At 10:40 A.M., I looked up from my book when the door suddenly swung open and Dr. Mullen motioned for Ben to go on out.

"We're done with the first part," Dr. Mullen said. "Ben needs a little break." Dr. Mullen opened the outer office door and smiled at Ben. "The bathroom is down the hall, first door on the left." Ben returned the smile and disappeared down the hall.

Dr. Mullen said, "Ben seems to be very comfortable. He's— " I didn't quite catch the last words because the muffled silence around us was suddenly broken by what sounded like a loud radio playing from the office on the other side of the reception room wall. In a moment, however, I realized it wasn't a radio at all, but instead Ben singing a favorite song, "When the Saints Go Marching In," at the top of his lungs from the bathroom.

"I'd say," I interrupted Dr. Mullen, "that Ben is completely comfortable. Do you hear him singing in the bathroom?" Dr. Mullen and I both had a good laugh, and within seconds, Ben had raced back to the reception room ready to go with Dr. Mullen for the next round.

By the time he and Dr. Mullen came out of the inner office at 11:50 A.M., Ben had worked up a good appetite. Dr. Mullen suggested that we take some time to eat our lunch while he evaluated the test results. When he went back to his office, I called Brian, and after dropping Jillian off at the neighbor's, he came right over. Before long, the three of us were sitting side by side at a desk, going over the test results with Dr. Mullen.

Shocking News

Dr. Mullen first reviewed briefly what the two tests were, beginning with the *Stanford Binet-Intelligence Scale, Form L-M*. He explained that it was the best tool he knew of at the time to use for a potentially highly gifted child. It had a higher ceiling than the *Wechsler Intelligence Scale for Children* (the WISC), which was more typically used by school psychologists to assess children ages six to 16.[4] A test ceiling is the top score that is achievable on that test. If the ceiling is too low, an individual can simply "top out" on the test, which doesn't reveal how high above the ceiling his or her intelligence actually is. The Stanford-Binet, L-M assessed Ben's ability to think in seven areas: language, memory, conceptual thinking, analytical reasoning, numerical reasoning, visual-spatial ability, and social intelligence. Ben's general performance on the test was measured cumulatively as an Intelligence Quotient score, or IQ.[5] Dr. Mullen began to explain what an IQ number meant.

"You need to understand how an IQ number reflects an individual person's mental abilities. There are two general ways of calculating the test score or IQ." For the first, Dr. Mullen explained how the IQ number reflects the comparison between a child's chronological age and his or her mental age.

"Let me explain this in basic terms," he continued at a steady pace. "Let's take, for example, three 10-year-old children. The first 10-year-old has the same chronological age and mental age, 10 and 10. His performance on the test would result in an

IQ score of 100. His mental abilities are right in line with the average 10-year-old.

"Now, take a second child. This child's chronological age is still 10, but he has a mental age of an average child of 12. His chronological age and mental age correspond to 10 and 12, reflected in an IQ score of 120.

"Now, take a third child and follow the same pattern. His chronological age and his mental age correspond to 10 and 14. He has the mental abilities of an average 14-year-old. He scores 140. A 13-year-old child with an IQ score of 130 has a mental age of 17. Working backwards for this situation: mental age (17) divided by chronological age (13) equals IQ score (130)."

I was fascinated with this relatively simple explanation of IQ scores. In the past, an IQ score was shrouded in mystery to me with no concept of relevance.

I wasn't the only one focused in thought. To my right, Brian was leaning ever so slightly forward, sitting attentively. To my left was Ben, his posture a mirror image of his father's. Dr. Mullen paused.

"I think I understand," I said. "So where does Ben fit into this?"

"Ben's IQ score is above the test's ceiling of 160. Projecting outwards, I've estimated his score to be somewhere around 170. He just turned seven, so his chronological age is seven years and zero months old. When you do the math, you find that the test score reveals a mental age of about 12 years old." Dr. Mullen paused at this point, allowing us to soak in what he had just said. "How does that sound to you two?"

"That sounds like Ben," I said. "He seems a lot like a sixth grader in the way that he talks about things and makes sense of things. He's comfortable hanging out with his older cousins... sure." I squeezed Ben's hand and smiled down at him. "That sounds like Ben." I responded with less surprise and more a feeling of comfort that our observations of Ben had just been validated.

"There's more. Remember, there are two ways of understanding IQ scores."

Dr. Mullen explained that to further understand the test results, we had to look at how a score deviates from the norm, or 100. "There are five standard deviations. Generally, the deviations are marked at 1=115, 2=130, 3=145, 4=160, and 5=180. The farther from the norm of 100, the fewer people there are with that score, as illustrated with a bell-shaped curve." As I was listening to Dr. Mullen's explanation of the deviations, the Richter Scale came to my mind when measuring the intensity of earthquake tremors. I was feeling inner tremors now, to think that Ben scored so high.

"So," Dr. Mullen concluded, "if you consider that 95% of the general population falls within two standard deviations below and above the average—that is, between 70 and 130, then Ben's IQ score is nearly five deviations from the norm. What does this mean in the frequency of kids like Ben? How many kids are there like Ben in the general population?" Dr. Mullen leaned slightly forward on his elbows, and his large dark brown eyes met ours. "Statistically speaking, how often do we meet a Ben Skinner?"

We held our breaths.

"Using a normal bell curve, we estimate that in every 100,000 children, there will be one child like Ben."

I was still holding my breath.

"Children who score even higher, at 180 or above, are likely one in 1,000,000," he said, filling the silence.

My eyes and breath were caught and frozen by his statement. It was as if I had a sudden shock. I was aware of a solid thumping beneath my ribs.[6]

"Wow," I gasped. I was blinking away tears that had unexpectedly gathered in my eyes. "Everything you've said up to this point seemed to describe Ben, but—but one in 100,000? I've always thought we'd find another child Ben would connect with, some other child he could relate to in the neighborhood or at school. I thought we'd come across someone who—" I felt the blood rushing to my hands and feet. "I see it's not that simple."

Dr. Mullen nudged the tissue box from the side of the desk to the front where it was within easy reach for me. Ben drew his body closer to mine, and I put my left arm around his shoulder. Brian gave me a firm, comforting rub and a pat on my back. We all continued to listen.

"Now for the second test. It's called the *Woodcock-Johnson Tests of Achievement.*" Dr. Mullen shifted in his chair. He told us that this test was commonly used in schools to measure achievement. It determined how Ben was actually able to perform in relation to concepts that are traditionally taught in school, such as reading, writing, mathematics, science, social studies, and the humanities. Dr. Mullen showed us samples of Ben's responses. His illegible handwriting and alien spelling were exactly what we'd been seeing in his schoolwork. The samples validated our concerns.

"Ben performed at the very beginning level of first grade for the reading, writing, and spelling. He came in at second to third grade for computation, and fourth grade for math problem solving. He seemed to be unfamiliar with the division symbols, so although he may have the potential to achieve here, his score may appear depressed because of a lack of exposure." Dr. Mullen stopped here. A new look of concern drew his eyebrows together, and the pitch of his voice elevated slightly.

"But when comparing his mental ability to his achievement, Ben is not performing anywhere close to what would be expected. He's performing anywhere from two to five grade levels below his mental ability."

At this point Dr. Mullen's voice, although elevated, remained calm, but his composure had changed. Each word became slightly emphasized with tense, urgent gestures.

"According to state special education laws, if Ben tested with an average IQ and demonstrated achievement two to five grade levels below that, he would require special education services for learning disabilities. As parents, you have a serious situation on your hands which must be addressed immediately."

During the rest of our discussion with Dr. Mullen, we clarified test scores and weighed the pros and cons of keeping Ben enrolled in Spanish immersion school. We also discussed the urgency of making a decision to implement changes in Ben's school day as soon as possible.

Dr. Mullen was clearly biased against keeping Ben in a language immersion environment. That environment had already proved to be less than helpful to Ben's reading and writing. His language performance was far below expectations, and Dr. Mullen believed that Ben would continue to suffer from lack of instruction in his native language.

"You have the responsibility to decide," Dr. Mullen told us. "What do you believe is more important right now: learning Spanish, or his overall intellectual development?"

We also had to take into consideration that the school was new; it had only completed two years of the Spanish immersion program. Currently, the program covered only kindergarten through second grade, which meant that there would never be teachers or curriculum available for Ben to access more than one year beyond his current grade level.

We all agreed that even if Ben's basic reading and writing language needs were addressed, the option to accelerate one grade level would not only prove complicated by the language barrier, there would be no opportunity for future advancement of any kind at this particular school.

By the time we left the office later that afternoon, the focus of our perceived challenge four hours earlier had taken a 180-degree turn. We were no longer concerned about making Ben's day more bearable by enriching his math program. We knew we had to think in terms of the bigger picture. The chasm between Ben's mental abilities and his academic performance was alarming. The concerns regarding math would take a lower priority for now. Our new, clearly defined perspective on Ben's abilities forced us to face reality. His enrollment in the Spanish immersion school would have to be completely re-evaluated.

Floodgate of Knowledge

I had done some reading on giftedness before Ben was tested, but now the topic had new relevance, and I pursued it with an insatiable passion. I checked out all of the books I could find in the library, of which there were too few, and searched the Internet for websites. I was looking for hard facts, yes, but I also was desperate to connect with others who could understand and empathize with our situation. I suddenly appreciated what an invaluable resource my mother would be. She loaned me books and referred me to literature, workshops, lectures, conferences, and many other sources that would help me understand the significance of Ben's high intelligence.

In the midst of my excitement, I couldn't resist the urge to share my newly gained knowledge with friends and acquaintances. However, to my chagrin, I quickly learned to keep my mouth shut and my thoughts and feelings to myself.

For example, a few days after Ben's testing, I attended a small meeting with three other women to discuss plans for the neighborhood winter party. We were all getting reacquainted over homemade cookies at the living room coffee table when two of the women left to check on the hot cider. Joan and I stayed and chatted.

She leaned forward and asked, "How is the Spanish immersion school going for Ben?"

This was a question I was used to answering because the school was new and different, and it generated a lot of curiosity. This time, however, my response diverted from the usual supportive statements. "It's actually been a real struggle lately. We're reconsidering what the best plan is for Ben at school. And," I paused, "we got him tested."

"Really?" She leaned even closer. "I know Ben is bright, but how did he do?"

"I'm still letting it all soak in. He hit the ceiling. He went over the top. He has the mental age of a sixth grader."

Joan was a pediatrician, so I expected her to be familiar with advanced development issues and respond supportively and professionally to the information. I was actually surprised by her response.

"Oh, gosh, Wendy." She straightened up slightly. With concern, she spoke in a low voice, "You'll have to be careful he doesn't get conceited."

The other women returned from the kitchen with cups of hot cider, and the general news of Ben's testing was shared and the topic changed, thankfully, to arrangements for hay rides and refreshments for the party.

I had mixed feelings about Joan's response. I was angry that she assumed Ben would become conceited if I weren't "careful." Ben was the most gentle and sensitive of boys, and he had handled the results of his testing with mature modesty. I also felt that her remark was insensitive and insulted me as a parent. Why couldn't she look beyond her nose to ask about Ben from a more compassionate angle? I would have preferred something like, "What does that really mean?" or "How does this affect your decision on school?" over a comment that assumed that Ben would get a big head.

I reminded myself that Joan was coming from a limited range of experience, and perhaps I'd put too high an expectation upon her. She was not only a pediatrician; she was also a mother of two young children. Being a pediatrician didn't mean that she was a psychologist, and a lot of what we learn about children comes from our own personal experiences with our families.

That evening, I learned two important things. First, I had to keep in mind that when I shared something with others, whether it was what we had for dinner last night or IQ testing, people project their own fears, needs, desires, and experiences into their responses. Second, if a pediatrician with two young children couldn't approach the topic with more grace and insight than Joan, I should expect few others to do any better. From then on, I was very careful about exactly how and to whom I spoke about our children and their giftedness.

Principal of Learning

Before Brian and I made our decision about Ben's school placement, we decided that we needed to meet with Mr. Swenson, the principal of Taft Primary School (K-3), the traditional public school Ben would attend if he left the Spanish immersion school. It was important for us to do some research before moving Ben from his school.

Having learned from our experience at the immersion school, I wanted to see who was in charge at Taft. Because the immersion school was only in its third year, it did not have a full-time principal due to the low enrollment of only three grades and strict budget constraints. I was unclear as to who called the shots and led the professional staff at that school. In considering this possible new school, we decided to look into the leadership skills of Mr. Swenson and to learn whether or not he would be supportive of Ben's unique learning needs.

We met after school on a Wednesday, one week after forwarding a copy of Dr. Mullen's formal assessment of Ben to Mr. Swenson. When we walked into his office, Mr. Swenson stood and greeted us with ordinary handshakes. On the credenza behind him were the usual framed pictures of family and children's artwork. There was also a glass aquarium with a black furry tarantula cozied up in one corner against a rumpled scrap of red flannel. Well, a pet tarantula was certainly unusual and something that would interest elementary-age children! After we all sat down, Mr. Swenson paused for a moment, his blue-eyed gaze through thick glasses poised on our faces for a brief instant, and said, "Well? You made the appointment. What's on your mind?"

I thought it was a rather blunt beginning. Mr. Swenson did not appear to be competing for Mr. Congeniality, but then, neither did he appear ready with his shield and armor either.

Throughout the conversation, Mr. Swenson's position was cautious and watchful. He was checking us out as much as we were checking him. We expressed our concerns honestly and openly, knowing that we had nothing to hide and certainly nothing to lose. By being transparent and forthright in that way, Brian and I thought we could trust Mr. Swenson's responses to be genuine and honest as well.

We discussed several topics: Mr. Swenson's professional background, the history of the teaching staff, class sizes and demographics, school philosophy in general, and how gifted kids fit into that philosophy, to name a few. By the end of our discussion, Brian and I were satisfied that we had learned three very important things: (1) Mr. Swenson had a clear vision for the school and was well supported by his staff, (2) he understood gifted children very well, and (3) he would do whatever was possible to meet Ben's needs.

Mr. Swenson was a tremendous supporter of public school education and believed that every public school had the responsibility to meet the needs of every student, from the least to the most able. He emphasized that he took that responsibility very seriously in his school in particular. He showed us that he walked the walk. With some flexible funding, he had implemented reading and math programs for children who needed the additional teaching to meet minimum standards. He personally taught a group of five gifted math students, beginning in kindergarten, for four years until they left after third grade to attend the intermediate school.

His performance record was comforting. As we learned that Mr. Swenson was a very intelligent—if not highly gifted—individual himself, we were even more convinced that this was the right place for Ben. It was apparent through not only Mr. Swenson's professional training, but also in how he expressed himself in our conversation. With his own personal background and his direct, meaningful contact through his teaching and administrative experience with gifted students, we felt that he understood our family's situation far more than anyone else had up to that point.

Mr. Swenson kept his objective distance in our discussion. He did not knit his eyebrows together and sooth us with obligatory words of sympathy. He challenged us by presenting us with as clear a picture as possible of his school, his staff, and his philosophy.

Yet in spite of everything Mr. Swenson discussed with us, a voice in the back of my mind kept nagging at me, "Will this be enough for Ben?"

As if he'd just read my mind, Mr. Swenson made a comment that jolted me to attention: "When a child scores unusually high on an IQ test, some parents assume that no school can meet their child's needs."

I had been walking on the edge of that assumption for some time. I'd seen other parents who were so frustrated that they'd pulled their gifted children from public school and schooled them at home. No doubt their children were exceptional, but I wondered if the parents' inability to negotiate with school personnel was a greater contributor to their dissatisfaction than their children's exceptional intelligence. To work effectively within the public school system is nothing I take for granted. A parent must be willing to learn from trial and error and seek advice from those who've jumped through the same hoops before them. Most importantly, when dealing with staff and administrators, a parent needs to develop a diplomatic approach that is collaborative instead of combative.

Some parents, for different reasons, find their situations too difficult and opt to directly control their child's education through home schooling. A number of these families meet the challenge of home schooling with shining success. Others find that they need more resources and opportunities from outside the home schooling network, and they return their children to public or private school.

I wasn't ready to cave in to my fears at this point, and I wasn't convinced that home schooling was the right choice for Ben at that time. Mr. Swenson's frank statement intrigued me enough to consider our public school option very seriously.

After Brian and I discussed the situation, we felt that Taft Primary School with Mr. Swenson (and his tarantula) would be a good fit. We appreciated Mr. Swenson's candid communication style, his ability to challenge us without patronizing us, and the way his personal actions demonstrated his underlying concern for the welfare of all children. Brian and I agreed; this principal was an instructional leader we could trust with Ben's educational challenges.

Painting

Although we were pleased that Ben might attend Taft School in the future, we still needed to deal with his current school situation. Our next meeting at the Spanish immersion school was an hour and a half conference with eight people in attendance, ranging from the top ranks of the school district to Ben's classroom teacher. Mrs. Klassen, the immersion school's part-time coordinator, did not have the authority to make a judgment in our case, so the oversight went directly to the assistant superintendent. Those who would be affected in any direct way attended the meeting: the program specialist and acting assistant superintendent, the district coordinator of gifted services, the K-3 gifted teacher, the coordinator of the Spanish immersion school, Ben's first-grade teacher, our private educational psychologist, Brian, and myself. The mix of those in attendance reflected the issue at hand: Ben's future education depended not only on his immediate classroom, but also on the ability of the school or even the district to meet his needs.

This time I was sitting in a grownup chair, as was everyone else. A serious grownup meeting, I thought to myself. As the eight of us crowded around a single large table in a spare room normally used as a faculty work and storage room, Brian and I sat at the far end. We all began to introduce ourselves. The introductions continued around the table in a clockwise direction and were respectful, accompanied by a few slightly nervous but welcoming smiles.

The hour and a half meeting was filled with free-flowing questions and answers, dotted with professional opinions and the sharing of past experiences. Most of the banter went back and forth between the assistant superintendent, the gifted coordinator, Brian, and me. Initial conversation revolved around a general explanation, and defense of, what Spanish immersion provided for children. This frustrated me because they were preaching to the choir. As a fluent Spanish speaker, I volunteered regularly in the classroom. Both Brian and I were on the school's policy board and attended Parent-Teacher Organization meetings. I understood and believed in the benefits of language immersion. But I couldn't help but realize that none of this had much relevance when it came down to Ben's individual needs, except that the very essence of the school's purpose—the acquisition of Spanish language through immersion—had acted as a significant barrier to Ben's progress.

Brian and I were not questioning the benefits of the school for most of the children enrolled. We *were* questioning whether the school or district had a policy that supported Ben's unusual individual differences. And if not, would it be flexible enough to make an exception to meet his extraordinary needs?

In addition to the lecture on the benefits of language immersion, the conversation remained stuck in a time warp. We couldn't get away from the present tense. Nothing was said about commitment to future possibilities, except that Ben wouldn't be able to accelerate to the next grade in math or any other subject at the immersion school due to the perceived language barrier.

"What about long-term needs?" I asked. "My concern is how any school with only one grade level above Ben's can meet his long-term needs." Before I realized it, my question was answered by another question, and the discussion took an entirely different course. My original plea for some sort of acceleration had disappeared into a black hole, and throughout the meeting, no matter how I rephrased my concern, no one ever committed an answer to it. Apparently, there was no answer.

"What about gifted education services?" I asked Mrs. Vanasek. "Can you explain how that all fits into the picture?"

"In February, Ben will begin seeing Tina Jansen with other identified gifted children in a small group for two to three hours per week in a pullout program."

"What about regular classroom hours during the rest of the day and week?" I asked.

Mrs. Vanasek sighed. "We have our hands tied when it comes to helping these gifted kids as much as they deserve. The State of Minnesota doesn't give any district money for gifted education. Fortunately, our district has chosen to support gifted education, but even then we are still understaffed compared to the need."

"I can understand that," I said, "but what about accelerating Ben in the near future? That wouldn't take any extra long-term time commitment from the gifted department. Would that be a practical option?"

Mrs. Vanasek responded in an exasperated voice, "Acceleration isn't always what parents hope it will be. It is not the all-in-one answer, Wendy. Acceleration can affect a gifted child in a terrible way if you're not very, *very* careful." Her voice intensified. "I've seen some kids do fine, but others have a hard time with social issues, especially feeling like they don't fit in." She paused and took a breath. "Social-emotional issues can't be taken for granted. When these kids grow older and become teenagers, some of them struggle with friendships, self-worth, a sense of belonging." Mrs. Banasek's last words weighed heavily in the air, and her animated gestures ceased as if the words had suddenly pinned her arms in her lap.

I was taken aback momentarily with her emphasis on the sense of belonging. It seemed to be a very real concern, as if she dealt with this aspect of gifted kids in the reality of her day-to-day work. Later, it reminded me of a story a friend had told me earlier when I had mentioned the possibility of accelerating Ben. My friend had said, "My brother was accelerated, skipped a grade, and he never recovered from all the teasing and struggles to fit in socially. He's brilliant, Wendy. And do you know what he does for a living? He's a painter—not to be confused with an artist. He paints houses."

At the time my friend told me about her brother, I couldn't help wondering how what happened to her brother had anything to do with Ben today. Many of the examples I was hearing seemed to be in the relatively distant past. And besides, Ben didn't feel like he fit in with his current school setting. Could it really be that much worse if he were accelerated?

During the full hour and a half, Mrs. Klassen, coordinator of the Spanish immersion school, was fully attentive, yet she never once spoke. This, I realized later, was probably, at least in part, a reflection of her precarious leadership position. She had been hired just three months prior to this meeting as a part-time coordinator, not a principal, and she had teaching responsibilities in addition to her highly demanding half-time administrative duties. Considering her silence, the decision-making power in the room was clearly not in her corner. Thus, although Mrs. Klassen was the highest ranking administrator in the Spanish immersion school, we could not depend on her to negotiate a policy to help Ben.

Dr. Mullen was surprisingly quiet as well; he spoke only briefly on two occasions that required clarification or emphasis regarding Ben's cognitive abilities. But his presence spoke more than words, and perhaps his economy of words was a positive sign that he felt Brian and I had a firm footing in the discussion.

Señora Cruz, Ben's teacher, said very little, but when she did speak at the conclusion of the meeting, her voice was strong and firmly committed. "I will do whatever it takes. I will work with Mrs. Jansen, and I will learn whatever I can to help Ben."

Throughout the meeting, the administration and staff shared many comments and anecdotal stories. They appeared to have the best of intentions. The assistant superintendent revealed that she had raised two gifted sons and had experienced many of the same frustrations and dilemmas we were beginning to encounter. Others shared their children's experiences with social issues that included bullying and exclusion, as well as the difficulty of finding challenging academic opportunities. Mrs. Jansen, the gifted and talented teacher, said she had raised three gifted daughters.

The anecdotal stories seemed to be intended to put us as ease, as if to say, "You're not alone. We empathize with your situation." But the unsolicited personal advice that accompanied some of these stories only exasperated me more. In this particular meeting, I didn't want their sympathy. I wanted professional, research-based, knowledge-based curriculum proposals to address Ben's needs.

We all agreed that Ben needed an immediate change, yet no one would give me a straight opinion as to whether or not the immersion school had the clear *ability* to meet his needs. Toward the end of the meeting, I couldn't contain my emotions any longer, and the tears flowed freely while Brian took up the slack. I was exhausted. I had asked as many questions and listened to as many answers as I could, yet I was left with the frustration of indirect discussion and no commitment to any specific plan of action. In spite of their genuine concern for Ben, no one would step up to advise us either way.

The district had recently adopted a new slogan: "Achieving success, one student at a time." I left the meeting believing that everyone in the room embodied that simple but meaningful statement. However, we each had our own idea of just exactly *how* we would help this one very different child. We all had distinct personal and professional experiences, as well as unique relationships, with Ben. Some in the meeting had never heard of him nor seen him, while others had known him for years. Fortunately, Brian and I had the ultimate say in the decision, and every individual in the room verbally or nonverbally assured us that they would support our decision. Unfortunately, the decision was heart-wrenching, and as his parents, we felt an enormous responsibility for Ben's successes or failures from that point on.

I told Brian later that night, "I already know about and agree with them on 90% of what they were saying about Spanish immersion and the challenges associated with accommodating gifted kids. It's just that it was so frustrating for me to listen to all this talk and still feel like we were moving against the current, like we aren't making any progress."

"Maybe they felt they had to say some of it," Brian said. "Maybe even though we already understood a lot of what they were saying, they had to say it for the record." Then Brian added thoughtfully, "Maybe they had to say it for themselves, Wendy."

Inhale and Exhale

I dialed the phone and took a deep breath. "Hello, Elena?… Yes, this is Wendy Skinner…. Fine, thanks…. Actually, I've had better days….Yes, Brian and I came to a decision. We've decided to move Ben to Taft, the regular K-3 school…." Big sigh. Sit down. "It's really the long-term outlook for Ben that's the driving factor."

Grab a tissue.

"I'm so sorry he can't stay at the Spanish immersion school…. I know I shouldn't apologize; it's just that we had such high hopes for him there. I'm so sorry….Thank you. Thank you for your support….Yes, we decided that we'd move Ben after the winter break. I think that's the easiest time to make the transition….I'll call the secretary at Taft and let her know, and to schedule a tour of the school for Ben…."

Exhale. Loosen the grip on the phone a little.

"Oh, Elena, thank you again....Will you tell Señora Cruz today?...And tell her I'll talk to her tomorrow at school when I come to read to the class....All right....You too....Bye...."

Hang up the phone. Take another deep breath.

Phone the secretary at the new school to notify her of Ben's enrollment.

Schedule a tour of the school with the secretary.

Telephone Mrs. Vanasek to accept the offer to evaluate Ben's math abilities over the next several weeks.

Now, stop, sit back down, and take another deep breath.

Phone Brian.

Tell him it's done.

# Chapter 4

Reading and the Yukon Song

With the decision to move Ben to Taft Primary School, the traditional K-3 school, it was as if I'd finally reached the platform at the end of a long tightrope with no safety net below in case of a fall. Our persistence and courage to take one step after another had paid off. Ben was on his way to a more positive school experience. However, we were soon to find that the tightrope act had only just begun.

Ben was happier. Once he was told he was moving to a new school, his disposition brightened. He was enthusiastic about touring the new school. When he peeked in on his new first-grade classroom, the teacher was showing answers on the over-head to an analog clock-reading exercise. The room was dim, and in the 10 seconds that we said hello, all the children's eyes were fixed on the doorway where the new kid stood. Ben and I recognized a few faces from nursery school and the early child-hood classes. Jennifer, a former member of Captain Ben's preschool police brigade, was there. Ben expressed a definite sizzle of excitement for his new school, which was becoming detectable in his positive attitude. Though he still lived physi-cally in the immersion school day-to-day, anticipation to move to the new school hummed just below the surface of his cool composure.

School began at Taft Primary School in January. Instead of waiting for the bus at our driveway, Ben and I walked up the street to catch the bus with three other neighborhood boys. There were the expected questions of why Ben was there, and after Ben's matter-of-fact explanations, they quickly accepted his presence. Ben now had several friends to sit with on the new bus. After that first day, he gave off the impression that he had ridden that bus since September.

He adapted equally quickly to his new classroom. "I keep forgetting that Ben is new to the class!" his teacher said when I called to check on her perception of how he was doing. "He fits right in, and he's renewed friendships with Ramon and Jennifer from preschool."

Ms. Schwartz was quick to recruit me for volunteer work an hour a week during the language arts. I was eager to be a part of Ben's classroom in order to get to know the school, the everyday class culture, and the other students. I spent every Wednesday morning helping a few of the children with their reading, writing, or spelling. Though I never helped Ben, I could see that he was determined to stick to the tasks of writing in his daily draft notebook, practicing his spelling words and improving his reading skills.

Ms. Schwartz's language arts time was structured, as was every first-grade class in the building, to support individual progress. Every child wrote something each day in a draft notebook using a two-step planning process of drawing a picture on the top half of the page, then writing the story to go with it on the bottom half. It was a simple organizational technique, but it was equally effective for the least skilled writer or the most advanced one.

The spelling program was two-fold. First, there was a basic set of high-frequency words that all first graders were expected to be able to spell by the end of the year. In addition, each child had his or her own set of weekly spelling words derived from the child's own draft writing. If a child used a word repeatedly and misspelled it often, then that word would be adopted for that child's spelling list of the week. The words were relevant and active in the child's language.

The element that most allowed Ben's reading ability to burst forth was a literacy-based reading program. Each child read at his or her own reading level independently by self-selecting a book from a bin with the appropriate level marked on it. Ben could clearly see where he fit in when he arrived in January. He was on level A, but not for long. In his classroom at that time, children at different stages were reading from level A through I, followed by chapter-style books, levels 1 through 3. Within a month, Ben had raced through levels A, B, C, D, E, F, G, H, and I.

This individualized and self-paced environment fed right into Ben's preference for the opportunity to set his own goals. Whenever he felt he was ready, he could approach the teacher with the current level book, read it aloud, and if he read with 90% or above accuracy, he could advance to the next level. This was an ideal system for a self-motivated little boy.

In class, Ben sat next to his old friend, Ramon. "Mom, Ramon is reading level 1 books," Ben told me one day after school. "I want to read level 1 books, too. I want to be reading them by the end of February." And by the end of February, Ben was reading level 1 books. But by then, Ramon had moved on to level 2.

Ben gave me another update early in March. "Mom, I think level 1 books are more interesting than those other levels like H and I. But Ramon is reading level 2 books, and there are more nonfiction books in that bin. They look even more interesting. I'm going to be reading level 2 books soon."

Ben was clearly delighted in his newfound power of reading. He had a revived interest in our collection of Calvin and Hobbes books and had found a page totally devoted to "The Yukon Song." Next to the title of the song was a drawing of the little boy, Calvin, wearing a helmet and a backpack, with his tiger following behind him carrying a toboggan. Each character's mouth was wide open with tongue showing, singing the praises of adventuring away from parents, authority, and rules.

After eating Easter dinner with my parents, sisters, brother, and their families, Ben pulled out the book, opened it to "The Yukon Song," and asked if we'd like to hear it. To a made-up, simple tune, he enthusiastically sang all nine stanzas, including, "We'll never have to clean a plate, of veggie glops and goos. Messily we'll masticate, using any fork we choose!"

Afterward, my father commented, "There's no doubt he's off and running with reading." By the next fall, merely nine months after switching schools and struggling with simple four-word sentences, Ben was reading *Harry Potter and the Sorcerer's Stone*, the first book in the ever popular series by J. K. Rowling. His new school was obviously a huge success for him.

Redundancy of Repetition Revealed

Ben's progress in reading was a great excitement, as well as a relief, of course, to Brian and me. Since attending his new school, his underlying anger and irritability had evaporated. We soon discovered that his unhappiness at his previous school was not merely an issue of academics.

"Mom, at Immersion, we did the same thing over and over," Ben confided to me after his second week at his new school. Over his after-school snack of peanut butter and crackers, he continued, "And I thought, when is this *ever* going to end? Never! Not until the end of first grade!"

It hadn't dawned on me until that moment how repetitive the nature of kindergarten and first grade must have been in the language immersion environment. Naturally. Repetition was necessary for most children to learn a foreign language, but it had become a ceaseless drone in Ben's mind. Add the drone of repetition to the simplistic nature of basic kindergarten curriculum, and no wonder Ben was so frustrated. I shuddered just thinking about the reality of this seven-year-old's hopeless expression of never-ending redundancy.

A week later, Ben shared his thoughts with me again. It was as if his brain had been incubating his idea on the bus ride home, and when he settled into his after-school snack, he came out with this remark, "I like the morning circle time with Ms. Schwartz, Mom. When we give each other the morning greeting, we pass a ball back and forth. Whoever has the ball says good morning to the next person they pass it on to. In Señora Cruz's class, the boys were not nice to the girls." Ben frowned. "They would only pass the ball to boys until they *had* to pass it to a girl. In Ms. Schwartz's class, everyone passes to everyone. It doesn't make any difference who you are."

These two episodes instantly reminded me of Ben's acute social and emotional sensitivity. He was very sensitive to justice and fairness, and his social environment was just as important to him as his academic environment. He had been unhappy with the social environment at his other school, but he hadn't known how to tell us.

Making Plans

Brian and I knew that moving Ben to the regular school was only the first step in finding a place where he belonged, both academically and socially. Once Ben settled in to his new first-grade surroundings, we scheduled a conference in March with his classroom teacher and the gifted teacher, Mrs. Jansen. The tightrope act continued with our guidance, though now we felt we had more of a safety net below us than we did six months ago.

At our first conference at Taft School, Mrs. Jansen opened the conversation with, "Let me begin by saying that I have never knowingly worked with a student who has scored so high on an IQ test. Working with Ben will be a learning experience for me and for everyone."

Wow, I thought. What a great beginning! I felt that some-body might finally be interested in understanding Ben and his needs.

Mrs. Jansen continued, "I still don't really understand what Dr. Mullen means by a 'mental age of 12 years old.' What exactly does that mean? I'm trying to make sense of that. Does it mean a bright sixth grader? Or…," she raised her eyebrows to finish the question.

Her question was so unexpected that I didn't have a clear and ready answer. But I thought that the answer was insignifi-cant when compared to the fact that a teacher for the gifted and talented didn't have a concrete understanding of basic IQ score interpretation. I didn't doubt that she had the ability to under-stand. Apparently, her training or exposure up to that point had never required her to nail down the significance of an IQ score and how that score related to average children of different ages. If a teacher for gifted and talented was fuzzy on understanding the significance of basic IQ test results, then how could I assume that a regular classroom teacher would have any idea what they meant or understand how to use this information in any way to help my child?

Because of Mrs. Jansen's acknowledgement that "working with Ben would be a learning experience for us all," I gained a new respect for her. I was beginning to see teachers in a new light—as growing, changing human beings who were continu-ally learning in their profession. These were people who could be formally trained in their field of expertise but still not know all the answers at every given moment.

To others, it may seem obvious that a teacher is human like anyone else, but a certain expectation of authoritative knowl-edge about children's learning and perfection in their field had always hindered my judgment to some degree. Previously, when faced with their imperfection, I had dismissed their credibility. But now I had to come clean and acknowledge the beauty regarding each person's individual experience involving my children. As we learn from each new encounter, our reactions are in constant flux as we aim for doing what is best for the child.

The conversation with Mrs. Jansen turned to Ben's general abilities in the classroom. Brian and I expressed our enthusiasm about Ben's progress, while Ms. Schwartz confirmed that Ben was advancing at a very rapid rate. The four of us agreed that placing Ben in a second-third mixed-grade class next year would be the best place for him.

"I know just the teacher," Ms. Schwartz said. "We should put him with Melissa Wright, who teaches one of the second-third multi-grade class teams. It's an arrangement where two teachers team-teach and share activities with both grades. They separate out into grade levels for reading and math. Melissa teaches with Lynette Roberts. They're a dynamic team—lots of fun. Melissa would be a great match for Ben."

"So if he were in this second-third-grade class, he could mix with the third graders and still have his second-grade friends?" I asked. Heads nodded. "And he could get a taste for the third-grade curriculum, and by the middle or end of the year, we could see if it'd be appropriate for him to skip to fourth grade the following year?"

A trace of concern knitted Mrs. Jansen's eyebrows together. "It's not often that we let children skip grades. We have to remember to keep Ben's social and emotional needs in mind, too. And then there's the issue of missing a year's worth of curriculum. Skipping or accelerating a grade is not always the best answer to meeting a gifted child's needs. We all have to keep a close watch on him next year and monitor how he's doing in every aspect."

"I understand your concerns," I said, "but Ben is such a mature little guy. I mean, sure, we do have to see how things go, but I have no doubt that he would adapt, and adapt happily. He's already learning and thinking about things way ahead of his classmates. I think he'll be very ready to move on." I paused and looked at Brian with a slight new apprehension in my voice, "But moving him into fourth grade after next year does sound a bit scary."

So it was decided. Ben would have Mrs. Wright for his teacher in the second-third-grade class, and we would wait and see about the grade skip. Brian and I heaved a deep and long mental sigh that afternoon. We could rest our concerns, for the time being, knowing that we had an appropriate and well-supported plan in place next fall for Ben.

Chapter 5

Libraries and Weight Lifting

As Brian and I met each of Ben's challenges with success, we were beginning to feel more balanced in our efforts and results. We were committed to learning from our experiences and hoped we could give Jillian the benefit of our first run through with Ben. However, leave it to Jillian to traipse through uncharted terrain. Early on, she made it clear that she wouldn't merely be driven down the trail; she would travel by her own creative and overtly self-determined means that occasionally required us to blaze an entirely new trail to accommodate her unique character and talents.

It's amazing how siblings can be so different. As a toddler and preschooler, Jillian challenged me in ways I never experienced with Ben when he was her age. Parenting strategies that had worked with Ben had little or no relevance or effect when dealing with Jillian. My approach to working with Jillian on cooperative behavior demanded a completely new set of skills, which included an interesting weight-lifting regimen.

When Jillian was an infant, trips to the library were spa-like mini-vacations of just the right combination of stimulation and relaxation. Ben and I would walk down rows and rows of books together, with Jillian in the car seat carrier. If we were lucky, she might be asleep, wrapped snugly and peacefully in her soft knit yellow blanket. When she wasn't asleep, she was still content to watch the dozens of mobiles slowly spinning from the ceiling or to track the other children passing by her with her bright and curious green eyes.

But these peaceful weekly trips to the library changed as she grew older. What used to be an easy and peaceful "carry-the-baby-out-to-the-car-and-go routine" changed into a "carry-the-screaming-toddler-out-to-the-car" routine. Jillian demonstrated a strong will—or stated another way, an increasing sense of self-determination. At this early stage of development, her determination far exceeded that of any other child I had ever observed.

I used all the strategies I knew. I gave her a five-minute warning, stated in clear language what I expected, and had plenty of crackers or Cheerios in the car to distract her. But Jillian was bent on directing her life in her own way and on her own schedule. I respected and admired her drive for independence, but I was not hesitant about enforcing my expectations when it came to the overall needs of the group.

One day in September, shortly after her second birthday, Ben, Jillian, and I spent a relaxing afternoon finding our weekly supply of books at the local library. After reaching our limit, Ben and I were ready to leave. Ben, who had a habit of distancing himself from confrontations, positioned himself just outside the library doors and waited patiently, anticipating the dreaded but by now familiar and inevitable scene that was to follow.

"Jillian, we are leaving in five minutes." I gave the warning in a level, even-toned voice. "I'm going to check out our books while you look at your book for a few more minutes; then we'll need to go."

"Okay," Jillian said without looking up from the picture book as her tiny fingers lifted a little paper flap that revealed one of Spot's lost dog toys.

"All right. I expect you to come with me when I'm done checking out our books. And remember," I touched her shoulder, "we have Cheerios in the car, too. All right?"

"Okay." Jillian's fingers discovered a red ball behind a flap hidden inside Spot's toy chest.

"Do you want to check out that book?" I thought I'd better be sure that Spot didn't complicate my exit plan.

"No," Jillian said in a calm and somewhat uninterested voice while she lifted a third flap revealing a bone behind a bright green bush.

"Okay. I'll check out these others and then we'll go." Just outside the doorway, Ben sat on the sidewalk intently paging through a large book with a toucan perched in a huge kapok tree on the cover.

Exit strategy so far going as planned. Ben was at his post, I had given Jillian the five-minute warning, announced in clear language what I expected, and notified her of the snack that awaited her in the car. Now the final step: actually leaving the library.

"All right," I said to Jillian, who hadn't moved from her chair at the tiny children's table. "Ben's waiting outside. We're ready to go."

"No. I want to stay," Jillian protested. "I don't want to go home."

"I know you want to stay, but we've stayed a long time already, and now it's time to go home." Then I said firmly, "Put the book back in the basket, Jillian."

"No!" She ignored me, with her eyes glued to the book and her fingers flipping several flaps at once.

"Jillian, if you don't put the book back in the basket and come with me on your own," I gave the ultimatum, "I will put the book in the basket for you and then carry you out."

"No!" Jillian screeched and went into escape mode, ducking under the table.

Within three seconds, I had 20 pounds of books in my canvas bag slung over my left shoulder and had extracted my 30-pound two-year-old daughter from under the table, holding her securely under my right arm. I made a beeline out through the doorway, ignoring stares from other library patrons, passing Ben, and heading straight for the car. Ben knew the routine. He picked up his book and followed me and my load like a faithful dog following a shepherd with a stray lamb in tow. Only instead of bleating, this lamb was screaming and kicking.

Dumping the book bag on the back seat, I wrestled Jillian into the car seat. Holding her chest firmly with my left hand, I buckled her in with the skill and speed of a hog-tying cowboy. Once she was secure, I checked Ben to be sure he was buckled in. Then, for the next eight minutes, Jillian raged in tears while Ben pressed both hands tightly over his ears. No one spoke a word over Jillian's screaming.

As we turned the corner onto our street, Jillian's crying suddenly stopped. She cleared her throat and took several much-needed deep breaths. Ben took his hands from his ears. I parked the car in the driveway, Ben quickly escaped with his book under his arm and raced up to the back door, and I unbuckled Jillian as she matter-of-factly reached over to the side of the seat and selected a handful of Cheerios from the previously ignored plastic container on the seat beside her.

She smiled at me, "These are yummy, Mama!"

"Okay, let's go into the house," I said in as normal a tone as I could muster.

"Okay!" Jillian enthusiastically responded as she hopped out of the car and hurried to join Ben at the back door.

Similar scenes happened with Jillian in the grocery store, at the park, and at home, just to name a few, and they continued for many months. She was ever true to her nature—that of strong-willed Jillian.[7]

Mittens and Sheep

"Time to go to the grocery store, Jillian," I announced. We'd cleaned out the refrigerator over the holiday, and after spending New Year's Day at Grandma and Grandpa's house, we couldn't put off grocery shopping another day. "Here, let me help you with your coat." Jillian poked her two-year-old arms through the sleeves of her thick winter jacket. I pulled her fleece hat over her head and ears and tied the flaps under her chin. Sitting on the top of the steps at the back door, she was unusually cooperative today, but something was missing in the ensemble.

"Oh! Your mittens!" I said as I spied two small mittens dangling on the ends of yarn strings coming out from the bottoms of her jacket sleeves. After I guided her hands into the mittens, I pressed them together and said playfully in a sing-song way, "You have two blue, nice, warm, wooly mittens!"

Her face transformed from an expression of passivity to one of sudden reflection as she focused intently on her mittens for a moment.

"Mama!" She looked up with a broad grin on her face. She held her hands straight out in front of her, displaying them clearly, and said, "I've never seen *blue* sheep before!" She watched me intently for my reaction, which was one of astonishment. Then she broke from her posture of display and laughed wholeheartedly at her own joke. "Blue sheep! Blue sheep!" she hooted five times over, laughing as she ran out to the car.

Boys for Friends

Jillian's first year of nursery school was her initiation into same-age group dynamics. At barely three years old, she was the youngest in the class, just having turned three two weeks before. With her gregarious disposition and uninhibited mastery of the universe, she quickly assimilated, developing friendships and adapting to the daily routine with ease. Her two best friends in preschool were boys, Cory and Luis, but her brother was always her first and best friend. By the time she was three, it was apparent that she had learned a great deal from him. With patience and uncommon tolerance of her emotional swings, Ben often played the role of coach, teaching Jillian about the give-and-take and joy of friendships and negotiation.

Our neighbor, Tony, was Jillian's next best friend. They often engaged in dramatic fantasy with complicated plots and detailed characters. High adventure in weird and mysterious alien worlds was usually a theme. Jillian and Tony, at age four, played all of the roles—actors, directors, scenery and props people, special effects engineers, and writers. As I listened to their chatter, I was reminded of a marathon-long play rehearsal. The director interrupted the actor to correct a scene, props were either added or taken away, and the script was written and rewritten to add another element of tension or surprise to the plot.

The actor and the director did not always agree, however, on the creative process, and this was where some of the real social learning took place. I was astounded by Jillian's expert negotiation skills she employed when trying to persuade Tony to let the aliens destroy the old city and rebuild a new city with the appropriate furry pillows and lightweight blankets. Sometimes Tony was unwilling to go along and held his ground. Then Jillian would switch tactics, and the two of them would come to a quick compromise to avoid any confrontation. I believe Jillian learned many of these skills while playing with Ben and was able to put them to the test as she played with Tony.

In kindergarten, Jillian remained friends with Tony, but as that friendship waned, she became good friends with Cory and Luis in her class. These boys clearly had in common a keen sense of humor and a compassionate sensitivity toward others, which Jillian appreciated. Later in the kindergarten year, Jillian told me how much Cory's sense of humor made her laugh and how much fun they had together at school.

Luis was a supportive friend as well. In the summer after kindergarten, Luis was on the same summer soccer team as Jillian. During one game, Jillian came to the sidelines in tears after taking a hard tumble from a collision with another player. Luis followed her and reenacted the scene with comical exaggeration in an effort to make her laugh. He couldn't bear to see his typically happy friend in tears and tried his best to bring a smile to her face with his silly vaudevillian antics.

Jillian never failed to gravitate toward active, imaginative, funny boys in her early years.[8] Occasionally, she had a girl friend over or played with a girl friend at school, but she made it clear early on that she was not interested in most typical girl activities—dolls, girl colors, girl clothes, or activities that most other little girls her age enjoyed. She preferred to actively involve herself with the company of boys who shared her enthusiasm for athletic pursuits or adventurous imagination.

Adam and Eve, and Santa Claus

When Jillian was nearly five, she became acquainted with Audrey. Audrey's parents both worked specific hours and couldn't manage a ride for Audrey to and from afternoon nursery school, so I offered to help with transportation. After several five-minute rides to school in the car and the time spent in school itself, the girls got to know each other well enough for Jillian to invite Audrey over to play one afternoon.

After a round of playing kitty with real milk in a saucer and real crackers for "cat food" in a dish on the floor, Jillian and Audrey were ready for some human snacks up at the table. I brought out peanut butter, crackers, sliced apples, and milk, and the girls happily accepted what I had to offer. While putting things away in the kitchen, I listened to their conversation in the dining room while they ate. My ears perked up when I heard the word "God" in reply to a question Jillian had posed to Audrey.

"God made me. My parents say God made me," Audrey answered as a matter of fact. "And God made the first people, Adam and Eve. We come from Adam and Eve."

"No," Jillian said, "I don't mean Adam and Eve. What I mean is where do you *really* come from, before that?" Jillian was fishing for a particular answer and trying to lead Audrey along in her thinking. Audrey was about to switch tracks. Jillian paused for a moment, then thoughtfully rephrased her question, "Where did *Adam and Eve* really come from?"

"God. God made them," Audrey repeated, a little irritated that Jillian hadn't listened to her better the first time. "At my church, they say God made Adam and Eve. They were the first people."

"No, people evolved," Jillian insisted. "The first people evolved from lower life forms. They evolved from one-celled animals. They *evolved*. We're made by our genes. Our genes evolve, and that's how we came from one-celled animals. Our genes *evolved*."

Audrey set her cracker down on her plate, looked dead on at Jillian, and pouted, "God made *me*, Jillian. And *God* made Adam and Eve."

It occurred to me that this was pretty serious stuff for five-year-olds, and I wondered if I should say something to change the subject.

"Your church is just telling you stories about God and Adam and Eve, Audrey," Jillian said in a frustrated huff. "They are just teaching you to believe in stories."

Audrey's hands had dropped to her lap, and her eyes teared up. I knew I had to intervene.

"Jillian and Audrey. Girls," I said, "let's not forget that many people believe many different things about God. Some believe in one god," I looked at Audrey. "Others believe in many gods, and others in no god." Now Jillian's eyes looked just as puffy as Audrey's. "People choose to believe or not to believe in God. That is their choice. It's not right or wrong."

A silence lingered heavily in the air after my last sentence. The girls were not looking at each other, nor did they seem the least bit interested in their snack any longer.

"Are you done with your snacks?" Two sets of sad eyes looked at me from the table. "Okay, here, I'll take your plates," I said in a cheery voice. "Jillian, weren't you going to show Audrey the basement? Remember all those cardboard boxes down there that we made into houses yesterday?"

Jillian immediately perked up. "Oh, yeah. Come on, Audrey. They're really cool. Let's go!" Jillian hopped off her chair, and

Audrey followed willingly. Relieved of the tense conversation of moments ago, both girls skipped down the stairs together and played happily without any more worries about personal beliefs.

That day and the next, I thought about the girls' discussion and how it might have seemed to each one of them. Jillian and Audrey were on completely different planes of reasoning. Jillian's logic must have seemed as foreign to Audrey as Audrey's faith in Biblical stories seemed to Jillian. And perhaps it seemed ludicrous to them to hear me say, "People *choose* to believe in God…and it's neither right nor wrong." Jillian's approach was based on what she perceived to be true. She could not grasp the idea that people who had a choice to believe in facts could choose to ignore them. In her context, if a fact exists, there is no choice but to believe it. Facts are as tangible and real as the daily rising and setting of the sun.

From Audrey's perspective, Bible stories were facts, too. Jillian's and Audrey's facts or beliefs at the age of five depended totally on the credibility of the sources of their information. Each believed completely in the legitimacy of her sources. The problem was that, at the age of five, neither girl had enough experience in the world to know that there are many different ways people think when it comes to questions of religion and philosophy. At five, most children still think in concrete terms and aren't yet ready for abstract reasoning.

While most children that age are not yet making a conscious effort to differentiate between fact and fiction, it was evident that Jillian was actively working it out in her own mind. As an avid fan of Greek and Roman mythology, she had placed the story of Adam and Eve in the same category as the story of Persephone's annual visits to Hades. One explained the origin of humans, the other the origin of the seasons. She was also aware of evolutionary theory and had experienced the life sciences first hand. After collecting and observing snails and mosquito larvae from the marsh pond behind our house; overturning stones to find millipedes, ants colonies, and beetles; and generally poking around for hours in the back woods, she was using personal experience and acquired knowledge to support her conclusions.

Going one step further, perhaps someday Jillian would ponder the possibility of incorporating tangible facts with faith, betraying neither one, but that day, the thought of accommodating both science and religion wasn't on her radar screen.

I admired her thoughtfulness and tenacity in defending her position. But Jillian demonstrated to me that afternoon that she was not yet emotionally prepared for the power of these well-developed attributes without the wisdom of some additional experience in the world and knowledge of the broad range of beliefs held by others. I would have expected such a conversation with a teenager, but certainly not from a child barely five years old.[9]

The Adam and Eve debate was not the last time that Jillian found her thinking in conflict with the early beliefs of other children. A similar discord occurred with Alexa, a first-grade girl more than a year older than Jillian who took violin lessons with her. The two girls had just finished their lesson. They lingered for a few moments while I waited outside the classroom in the hallway with Jillian's violin in hand. I didn't hear the seemingly innocent conversation between the two girls completely, but I could tell it involved a discussion of Santa Claus. Jillian told Alexa that she knew there was no Santa Claus, and Alexa, with a smile on her face, walked over to her mother.

"Mommy," Alexa said in a bright voice, "Jillian says there's no Santa Claus. But *I* told her he comes to our house every—"

"Don't tell Alexa that, Jillian!" Alexa's mother scolded, in a panicked, angry voice. "That's not *nice*! Don't tell Alexa that!"

Alert to the tone of voice I heard from within the classroom, I looked through the doorway. Jillian trailed Alexa and tried to take back whatever she had said. Although she spoke in a gentle and explicatory voice, she only managed to dig her hole deeper. "Alexa, some people *do* believe in Santa and some—"

"Jillian! *Stop* that!" Alexa's mother spoke sharply and stepped between Alexa and Jillian. Alexa's mother stood toe to toe with Jillian. Then, stooping, with her face uncomfortably close to Jillian's face, she continued to admonish Jillian in front of Alexa and everyone else in the classroom and hallway. "Santa Claus is *real* to Alexa. That's not *nice* to tell her he doesn't exist."

Alexa's mother continued to rave. Jillian rushed to me with tears rolling down her cheeks. She grabbed my sweater tightly and buried her face in it as she sobbed. Alexa's mother followed her out into the hall, still lecturing. I was furious. Couldn't this woman see that Jillian had intended no harm and that she was overwhelmed by the unexpected intrusion into her conversation with Alexa?

I said, "I don't think Jillian meant any harm."

I grabbed the violin in my left hand, scooped up Jillian with my right, and headed down the hallway without looking back. My eyes burned. I tried my best to comfort Jillian without revealing my own rage as we left the building and got into the car.

I clenched the steering wheel as I backed out and started for home and said, "Jillian, kids who still believe in Santa Claus are sensitive about others telling them he doesn't exist. And the same goes for their parents sometimes." Jillian blurted out with a new round of tears, "I tried to tell her that *some* people believe in Santa Claus and *some* don't."

Looking back at it now, I realize that Jillian was applying a previous statement I had made to a new situation. When she and Audrey had disagreed about God and Adam and Eve, I had said, "People choose to believe or not to believe. That is their choice. It's neither right nor wrong." Apparently, she'd made the leap from God to Santa Claus—two beliefs which, at her age, were indistinguishable from myth and faith.

"I know you did, honey." I reassured her. "You didn't even have a chance to finish talking about it with Alexa. I know you weren't trying to be mean." Her crying gradually subsided to a sniffling quiver. I said, "It's just that some parents are very protective of their children, and I am *so* sorry in this case that Alexa's mother was angry with you."

I explained that I was upset because I thought Alexa's mother should have talked to her own daughter about how to handle differing opinions about Santa Claus instead of yelling at Jillian. I felt it was wrong that the girls' innocent conversation was abruptly spoiled by a panicked adult.

I reached back and handed Jillian a tissue. "Jillian, we all have to remember," I told her (but it was more of a reminder to myself than to Jillian), "that when we express our opinions, we must do so respectfully. People have their own ideas, just like you do. Sometimes their ideas are different from yours. When you tell someone you don't believe in Santa Claus or the Tooth Fairy or the Easter Bunny, you have to respect what they say, whether you agree or not. Because it's what they believe," I took a tissue for myself, "even if they get angry with you."

Vivaldi

When Ben was about three years old, I borrowed a couple of cassette tapes of classical music composer stories from my oldest sister. The stories interwove each composer's music with an adventurous story, mixing together history, fiction, and classical music. The composers included Beethoven, Bach, and Handel, as well as the one who later became our favorite, Vivaldi.

Ben made it clear at three that he didn't like the Beethoven tape because it was too sad and too scary for him. In the story *Mr. Beethoven Lives Upstairs*, a young boy, whose father has recently died, is confronted with what appears to be a raving mad Beethoven who rents a room in the upper floor of his home. It was typical for Ben to avoid scary stories in the form of books, tapes, movies, television, even radio, regardless of how happy the ending. It seemed to me that his empathic abilities to relate to the characters were so strong that it smothered all his hope for a happy ending. His heightened emotional duress did not allow him to wait until the end of a story to experience the resolution of conflict. This made it unbearable for him to listen to or watch a dramatic presentation on tape or in the movie theater.[10]

Jillian, on the other hand, though equally sensitive, early on found an inner strength and hope for the protagonist to overcome his or her conflict that allowed her to endure until the tension was resolved.

When Ben was only three, Brian and I made the huge mistake of taking him to see his first movie, *The Lion King*. Since it was a Disney movie and rated G, we thought it would be fine for a three-year-old. But not *our* three-year-old. The death of the father lion in an intentional stampede and the cruelty of the evil hyena entourage were emotionally devastating and frightening for Ben. The sensory overload of the stereo speaker music, sound effects, and the grand scale visuals only added to his fright. It became an inescapably overwhelming experience. The entire film upset him so much that from then on, we had to be especially careful to pre-screen whatever he was exposed to. We didn't bring him to a movie theater again until he was eight years old.

When Ben was seven, he experienced emotional pain when I read him *The Incredible Journey* by Sheila Burnford. I loved reading books out loud to the kids and would give the different characters different voices, evoking my dramatic talents in as realistic a manner as possible. Once again, I made an erroneous assumption. I thought, this is the great classic story, just like I remembered from my childhood. Three endearing animal characters—a roguish English bull terrier, a rambunctious golden retriever, and an indomitable Siamese cat—are lost in the Canadian wilderness hundreds of miles away from home, and eventually, after many adventures, they miraculously find their way back. An excellent book to read aloud, right? Not for Ben. In a sudden burst of tears, he begged me to stop when I began reading the account of the young golden retriever's encounter with a porcupine and subsequent painful injuries.

I felt guilty for weeks afterwards, shaming myself for not having had the sense to read through the book beforehand with an eye for Ben's sensitive nature. Ben didn't let me forget it, either, and to this day, he will not read either *The Incredible Journey* or *Where the Red Fern Grows*, another story with a dog as the central hero who ultimately dies doing what he loves doing best, catching raccoons.

To my great relief, the Vivaldi story proved to be a story Ben loved. Vivaldi's *Ring of Mystery* is a tale about an Italian girl named Katarina who is mysteriously orphaned as an infant in a shipwreck and who, years later, discovers her true identity. Katarina learns to play the violin with the nuns in the hills of Northern Italy and is eventually sent to a girls' orphanage in Venice. There, she joins the school orchestra with the amazing Antonio Vivaldi as the teacher and conductor. The end of the story reveals that Katarina is actually the long lost granddaughter of the duke, and she is reunited with her family. Throughout the story, beautiful music from Vivaldi's "The Four Seasons" dramatically sets the mood for each scene.

The first night Ben listened to this story, he was in his bedroom with the door open, and I was working at my computer just outside and around the corner. Ben was listening intently to the tape, and when it stopped, I heard him sobbing. I got up from the computer, went to his room, and sat on the bed beside his little body.

"Ben, what is it?" I asked, thinking that someone had surely died a tragic death in the story tape. I silently scolded myself again for not having listened to the tape before Ben did. "Did someone get hurt? What is it, honey?"

"No. It's that the story is so beautiful," Ben sobbed, wiping his tears on his pajama sleeve. "I have to listen to it again." He pressed the rewind button and settled into his bed again, suddenly oblivious to my presence. I left his room, curious as to what exactly happened in the story that had touched him so profoundly. I returned to the computer and continued my work.

It was 10:30 P.M. now. An hour had passed, and again I could hear Ben sobbing. He came out of his room with the tape player in his hand and approached me.

"Ben, hey, honey. What is it? Please, tell me why you're crying," I gently begged Ben. "What happened in the story?"

"Mom, Katarina found her grandfather. She wasn't alone anymore." He paused and repeated, "She wasn't alone anymore. She found her grandfather." Ben's seven-year-old face was a contradiction. His eyes were wet and red, and yet he had a peaceful smile from his lips to his eyes. After my brief inquiry, Ben rattled off the following questions and comments. He was bursting with thoughts.

"Mom, can I learn to play the violin?"

"Can you check out more opera tapes?"

"You get the most beautiful music tapes."

"I love you."

Ben's face was flush and his eyes wide. He took a deep breath and returned to his room. He didn't get to sleep until 11:30 that night.

The next night, it was Jillian's turn to listen to the Vivaldi story, and although she did not emerge from her bedroom with tears of joy, she *had* to listen to the tape again. And again. And again. Every night for months afterwards she listened to that tape before falling asleep. Although Ben had originally asked to play violin (he later chose to play the accordion because of its complexities), Jillian was the one who persisted in asking for violin lessons. Per her request that fall, Jillian began playing violin, just like Katarina.

There was something going on in Jillian's mind that was strikingly important to her during her nightly bedtime listening ritual. She insisted on having her blinds down, lights off, and her door closed—quite the opposite from Ben. In her darkened room, she would bury herself under multiple layers of blankets and rest her head on three thick pillows. Then she would turn on the tape and play the performance out in her head, in the darkness, over and over and over.

Searching the library for more high-quality story tapes, I found some beautifully narrated short stories, as well as novels. Our library system has an online catalog that makes finding new material fun and easy. The site includes book lists sorted by award winners, best sellers, age groups, genres, topics, etc. You can also search for a book by using keywords in the title or the text. In addition, there is a cross-referencing system that will show you each subcategory under which a book is listed. By selecting these subcategories, you can find other related books. Besides an easy-to-use and in-depth library catalog service, nothing worked better for finding good stories than asking cousins and other friends what they were reading. Word of mouth between families of avid readers often led us to books we might not otherwise have considered.

After discovering Vivaldi's *Ring of Mystery*, there were several other music story tapes that Jillian listened to repeatedly over the summer, including American Indian, Cajun, and Irish tales of mystery and legends. Then, in the fall of first grade, came *The Arcadians* by Lloyd Alexander, a book told in traditional Greek myth style with strong female characters and cutting humor. That Halloween, at the age of six, Jillian made her own costume accessorized with a macramé of scallop shells and beads attached to the end of a carved wooden walking stick. She was dressed as the Lady of Wild Things, the main protagonist in *The Arcadians*.

Next, Jillian discovered *The Story of Dr. Doolittle* and *The Adventures of Dr. Doolittle*. For months, she listened to these stories that were narrated by an older British actor with a delightful accent. After the Dr. Doolittle books, she discovered the *Redwall* series by Brian Jacques, with wild animal characters from the English countryside battling their foes in a King Arthur-like era, complete with castles and chivalry. Three of the dozen or so books in the popular series were on tape: *Redwall*, *Martin the Warrior*, and *Mossflower*. Within a week, Jillian listened to the first six tapes of *Redwall*, then the next eight tapes of *Martin the Warrior*, and finally the last 10 tapes of *Mossflower*. Just as before, she listened over and over to the tapes before falling asleep. But this time, instead of imagining the canals of Venice, she watched the mice and badgers battling wildcats and weasels at the castle gates during a private performance in the theater of her mind's eye.

Listening to these stories involved a high level of visualization of every detail. For one of the *Redwall* books, Jillian made a graphic record of the story's events in a tiny spiral notebook. One scene went on for several pages and detailed a heroic mouse fleeing a villainous snake through a tangle of underground tunnels. Jillian kept a running interpretive sketch, mapping the maze of tunnels and indicating through tiny M's, S's, and directional arrows the sequence of events all the way to the climax, when the mouse kills the snake in a tall vertical shaft. Each time she replayed the tape, she traced the diagram as if the action was taking place right under her fingertip on the page as Brian Jacques' British voice described it.

By the time Jillian was seven, she didn't wait for Brian Jacques to put out the next audio edition of the *Redwall* series. She made a list of all the books in the series published up to that point, and like notches in a shotgun, she crossed off each succeeding book as she read it. When she had read all 14 books on the list, she returned to her favorite titles and re-read those. Her intense audio training had primed her pump, apparently, for the reading of more complex, lengthy novels. She read *Alice in Wonderland* at seven and loved it, and at eight years old, she read the original English translation of *The Book of 1001 Nights*, otherwise known as *The Arabian Nights* by Sir Richard Francis Burton. Nothing would stop her now!

Throughout the children's school years, we took full advantage of the public library. A new supply of books and tapes kept my children's love of learning alive through many years of schooling.

Chapter 6

Eight-Year-Old Heaven

After what had become by now our standard routine of pre-conference discussion, defense buildup, and strike initiatives, Brian and I thought we were well prepared for Ben's second-grade fall conference.

"Hello, Wendy," Melissa said as she shook my hand. She extended her hand to Brian. "I don't think we've met."

"Hi, Mrs. Margoles," Ben said and added his own hand to the procession of handshaking with his teacher.

Mrs. Margoles was always Melissa to us and most of her students from day one. She preferred it that way, and Ben appreciated the equality of a first name basis. After a brief casual chat, we all sat down at the classroom table. Brian and I were ready to present our case for advancing Ben in math into the third-grade group. For this conference, we'd decided to start small and then build up our expectations as we established a relationship with this new teacher.

"Before we begin," Melissa said, "I need to discuss with you something that will have an impact on the rest of the conference."

Brian and I looked at each other. Where was this teacher taking us? She explained, "I spoke to Tina Jansen, the gifted teacher, and I understand that you've discussed your daughter Jillian's possibility of accelerating. As for Ben, I'm recommending that he accelerate as soon as possible to third grade."

Knowing that this was what Brian and I had thought would ultimately be the best fit for Ben, I squeezed Brian's hand under the table approvingly.

"Of all the children I've taught in the past 15 years," Melissa continued, "I've never seen a more appropriate situation for acceleration. Ben fits every criterion for grade skipping. He's already mastered all of the second-grade reading, writing, and spelling, as well as the math goals that I'd expect second graders to know by the end of the school year. Socially, he's mature, well-liked by his peers, a leader in his own quiet way, confident, and overall very happy and well-adjusted. There couldn't be a better time or a better classroom situation in which to move him up to third grade. With the advantage of the multi-grade classroom, he'd get to stay in this class with me." She paused with a mock pout directed toward Ben. "The only drawback is that I wouldn't get to have Ben for a second year like the other second graders."

The conference continued with particular details regarding Ben's acceleration and concluded in agreement with another set of handshakes all around.

That evening after both children were in bed, I said to Brian, "Do you realize that this conference was the first time we didn't have to explain or defend Ben? That for once, the teacher was *ahead* of us? Incredible! What a relief. What an amazing sense of relief!"

"And she's a class act, too," Brian added. "She's got a lot of teaching experience, and she's training to be a principal. I like her straightforward communication style. She seems to understand what's going on with Ben, and I trust her."

Ben's conference was on October 17th, and on October 28th, his eighth birthday, he moved from the second-grade to the third-grade group for language arts and math. In addition, he moved into the third-grade gifted pullout program. I spoke with Melissa after the second day of the official shift. She said that when she announced to the class that Ben would be joining the third graders' languages arts and math groups, all of the children let out a spontaneous cheer accompanied by wild applause for Ben. It was as if Ben had just scored a goal for the home team and his teammates were cheering him on.

For several days after this event, Ben ran to the bus stop, ran home from the bus stop, ran up the stairs, and ran down the stairs. He kissed me, his dad, his dog, and even his sister. He went to bed late. He woke up early. In the space of one week, Ben had turned eight and become a third grader. He had flown up to heaven and wasn't coming down anytime soon. His abilities and potential had at last been acknowledged. He felt encouraged and supported, not only by the adults in his life, but by both his old pals in second grade and his new friends in third grade. To top it all off, now he would have more challenging work in spelling, in reading, in his gifted class, and in what he loved most of all—math.

A New Country

Even with all of Ben's joy and excitement over his promotion to third grade, he still experienced a sense of loss over officially leaving his second-grade peers—especially the gifted class called Challenge. On his own initiative, Ben wrote a sweet goodbye letter and asked Mrs. Jansen to read it to the second-grade gifted class.

> *Dear Challenge Friends,*
>
> *I'm sorry I'm not going to see you in Challenge anymore. I will miss you. You are good friends. Have a great year!*
>
> *Your friend,*
> *Ben Skinner*

As I pulled the covers up under his chin that night at bedtime, Ben said, "I'm kind of sad to leave my second-grade friends in Challenge. But at the same time," he paused with a hint of self-imposed guilt hanging in his voice, "I'm not sad."

He rolled over and patted the bed beside him.

"Is it like leaving home to live in another country?" I asked as I sat down on the bed. "You're sad to leave home and all your friends, but at the same time, you're excited to live in another county and to learn different things and meet new people. Is that what it's like?"

"Yeah, it is," Ben nodded while smiling to himself, his chin brushing the red bedspread.

"Well, nothing to feel guilty about. We're all excited for you." I touched his forehead lightly. "I think you'll feel right at home in your new country."

A Fourteen-Year-Old Heart

Media has long portrayed the smartest kids as geeks and social outcasts. The intelligent male character is a nerd who wears thick glasses, can't hit a baseball to save his life, and finds that all the girls make a point of avoiding him around homecoming and prom season. Other students befriend the lonely geek only to abuse his friendship and convince him to share his answers to the math exam behind the teacher's back.

Most of us believe some form of these stereotypes, especially those of us who grew up with National Lampoon's *Animal House* and Disney's *The Absent Minded Professor*. But gifted children—girls and boys—come in just as wide a variety of backgrounds and characters as the general population. Many gifted kids have numerous talents and interests and aren't the least bit nerdy. Sure, there are a few kids who fit the nerd profile. But there are plenty of others who are gifted academically and are also skilled athletes. Some are social leaders. Still others excel in an area of talent like music, art, writing, or computers. Some shine in one area of talent, while others display multiple talents. And to complicate things, some kids appear to have big discrepancies within themselves—that is, to be slower than usual in one area while far ahead in another. In fact, some are gifted in one area and also have a learning disability in another.

An earlier way of thinking was that this last group of children couldn't be gifted because they were below grade level in something, even though they were far ahead of their peers in other areas—for example, the fourth grader who writes chapter after chapter of elaborate fantasy with complex plots and characters but who can't tell you the times tables. Or another fourth grader who can do three-digit division in his head but can't write a complete sentence. Today we call these children "twice-exceptional." They need and deserve special help in both areas—both the learning disability area and the gifted area.

All gifted children have unique academic needs. And some have weak areas along with their strengths, which need to be addressed. What's important is to realize that there is a huge variety and range of talents and abilities within the gifted population, and the same type of program is not necessarily appropriate for all.[11]

Social maturity within the gifted population is no different. Some kids appear dramatically immature when compared to their intellect, and others are sensitive and mature for their years. And being gifted and talented doesn't stop with academic areas like math and reading. Even at a very young age, some gifted children will show an acute sense of empathy and caring, social justice, and concern with fairness, whether they are interacting with adults or their age peers.[12]

A niece of ours demonstrated this gift for empathy and leadership as early as first grade. After her father read to her about the little hobbits protecting their shire from the monstrous orcs in the *Lord of the Rings* trilogy, by J.R.R. Tolkien, the girl used this model to organize a successful anti-bullying force on the playground at school. Later, in her middle school years, she discovered the histories of Nelson Mandela and Mahatma Ghandi and adorned her room with cutouts of their photos and articles on human rights struggles. In high school, she was president of her Amnesty International student group, an international human rights organization. Now, as a young adult, she works as an advocate in a homeless shelter. When people meet her today, they quickly recognize her gifts in the area of social justice, but would they imagine that she began to act upon this interest and talent at the young age of seven?

Our son, at age eight, seemed advanced in still another interesting social area. It was not social justice, but rather social interaction with girls. He was very interested in socializing with girls, almost as if he were a teenager.

"Mom, are we going to the neighborhood Halloween party on Saturday night?" Ben asked as he stirred the marshmallows in his hot chocolate on a chilly autumn evening. He had celebrated his eighth birthday the day before, and now Halloween was just around the corner.

"Yes," I replied, placing a small plate with toast and homemade grape jelly down next to his mug of hot chocolate. "We're all going. It starts at seven at the Peterson's house."

"Can people who aren't from the neighborhood go?" Ben paused, "I mean, if they're invited?"

"Sure, if they're a guest, a friend of someone in the neighborhood," I said. "I don't see why not."

"Then can I take Vanessa to the party as my guest?" Ben asked.

"Sure. That would be a very nice invitation. I'm sure she'd be happy to come. And be sure to let her know she needs a costume. Why don't you call her right now?"

Before we left for the party, I asked all three kids to come into the living room for a photo. The costumed children came racing down from the upstairs bedrooms: Ben, a handsome pirate with a penciled thin curling mustache and a golden hoop earring; Jillian, a stunning woodland fairy with long frizzy golden hair framing her exaggerated eye-lashed eyes; and Vanessa, a loveable shaggy black and white cat with pink circles for cheeks and long black painted whiskers. Posed on the sofa, the eight-year-old pirate and his five-year-old sister-fairy flanked their cat friend on each side. It was the best Halloween costume photo I ever took. All three kids had the bright sparkling eyes and broad smiles of children anticipating this exciting night.

As I drove home after the party, Vanessa and Ben sat together in the far back seat of the van and carried on a conversation filled with "next time," "my house," and "your house."

About six weeks later, I found a flyer in our front door for another neighborhood party. This time, a horse-drawn hay wagon would transport carolers around the block. Ben wanted to again invite Vanessa, but unfortunately, she was sick and would not be well enough by Saturday night's gathering.

Ben didn't let his disappointment stop him from implementing Plan B. He immediately asked if he could invite Katelin instead. Katelin rode on the same bus as Vanessa and lived only a few houses away from her. He knew Katelin from his second-grade gifted and talented pullout group. She was a spunky, dark-haired, dark-eyed girl who could easily hold her own in any group—girls or boys. So on that moonlit winter night, Katelin was Ben's guest as they sat on hay bales with blankets across their laps, had snowball fights, and feasted on popcorn, cookies, and chips with the other neighbor kids in the basement of the party host's home.

Then, in January, Ben spent nearly two nights on the computer carefully crafting a love letter for Vanessa. He wrote "I love you" on the front, and inside, "#1 Vanessa, #2 Katelin." He intentionally mailed the card instead of giving it to Vanessa at school. In his P.S., he wrote, "I apologize if this card embarrasses you." Ben explained to me that mailing it would avoid further "embarrassment" because the other kids at school "just wouldn't understand."

In February, Ben went so far as to spend his own money at Target for a Valentine gift for Vanessa—a gold chain with a golden heart pendant. Vanessa sent Ben a thank-you card that read, "Thank you for the necklace. I love it so much. Love,

Vanessa," and enclosed her school picture. The next morning when I was in Ben's room to wake him for school, I noticed something new. The card and Vanessa's school picture were taped, front and center, to the cupboard door of his desk. It seemed we had an eight-year-old boy with a 14-year-old heart.

The 10/90 Rule

Minnesota began implementing new graduation standards the year Ben began third grade. One of the standards to be newly assessed that spring required third-grade students to demonstrate how well they understood structuring a piece of writing to include a beginning, a middle, an ending, supporting details, and mechanical accuracy.

Ben fretted about this task with a worry and anxiety that perplexed us. We knew he was capable of thinking and expressing himself with great verbal precision and organization, so we couldn't understand why he had such an aversion to transferring his thoughts to written words on paper.

"Just talk to yourself, Ben, and then write what you say. We could even let you use the tape recorder as a tool," I said, lightly tapping the crown of his head. "We know you've got it up here."

"But Mom," Ben nearly cried, "I just can't do it. I just can't. I don't know what to write about. I just can't write!"

As it turned out, Ben's anxiety wasn't a reflection of his ability to execute the writing assignment. Rather, he was acutely sensitive to criticism of his writing and took any critical comment as a personal attack. And no wonder. Every time he wrote, his dad or I would ask to read his work in order to monitor his progress. No matter how well anything was written, because of our own perfectionist tendencies, we always had some word of advice or a tip to improve his efforts. Ben struggled with his desire to seek our approval by showing us his work, and yet he was paralyzed by the fear of our well-meaning but critical responses. And paralyzing it was indeed. It seemed the more we encouraged him, the less courage he could muster to expose himself on paper.

How did Brian and I come to recognize the part that we played in this predicament? After some discussion one night, it dawned on both of us that Ben was showing a similar pattern of reluctance to write as he had to reading aloud when he'd been in first grade. Was there a common thread in these two experiences? Yes. Every time Ben read or wrote, I, his mother—his involved and very interested mother—was demanding a performance of sorts. Yes, I had to admit that sometimes I reacted to each word read or written by my children as though it were a performance. And these performances were judged by an audience that gave a rating demonstrated by an applause-o-meter: boos, whistles, smiles, and frowns. I needed to lighten up and give my son a chance to breathe. He needed to feel free to express himself purely for the pleasure of it without ratings or evaluation from me or others. When gifted children demonstrate their precocious talents or skills, it is all too easy for parents (as well as grandparents and teachers) to set them up for the performance trap, the applause pitfall, where they feel they must always perform well. Helping our children escape this trap can only happen when we recognize the power of our words and then use them with sensitivity to our children's emotional needs.

To compound his anxieties, Ben was afraid not only of us reading his work, but of anyone else reading it as well. He held his thoughts and feelings very dear—even sacred. To him, whatever he wrote on paper needed to reflect those thoughts and feelings. He could only write what was important, worthy of recording, and therefore deeply personal. He wouldn't write a simple, imaginary story if it seemed irrelevant or petty to him. In fact, he refused to write trivial material to satisfy the requirements of an assignment. Exposing his personal thoughts and feelings to others only to come up short in some way or be inadequately expressed horrified him.

Some reading samples from Ben's third-grade daily journal show a few different aspects of his writing style. He rarely elaborated, in spite of his teacher's encouragement. Most often he was straight, terse, and to the point, apparently seeing no need for extra explanation or elaboration. Teacher prompt: *At the end of winter break, you had about nine hours of daylight. Now you have more than 13 hours of daylight. What are you doing with your extra daylight?* Ben's response: *I am probably going to play Monopoly.*

He also was brutally frank. Teacher prompt: *If you knew that you would have a snow day tomorrow, what five books would you check out of the library?* Ben's response: *"You can't predict the future. But…I'll answer the question anyway. 1. The Snowy Day, 2. The Night Before Christmas, 3. Encyclopedia Brown Book 21, 4. E.B. Book 20, 5 E.B. Book 19."*

On one occasion, perhaps after a less than eventful day, he did elaborate a bit. Teacher prompt: *If you could place your desk or table any place in the room, where would you put it, and why would you move it there?* Ben: *In the coat room because it is harder to hear the teacher. That way it's easier to not hear boring subjects.* His teacher then wrote: *Like what?* Ben didn't answer her question.

Ben finally chose to describe a personal experience for the third-grade graduation standard writing assessment. He had many false starts with no finishes until finally, at the eleventh hour, he stayed in from recess to complete his writing one day before the deadline. He had procrastinated as long as possible to avoid the dread in the pit of his stomach. It was at that time that Brian and I decided we would exert as little pressure as possible on Ben regarding his writing in hopes that it would free him to be more responsible to himself and less responsible to us. Days later, at Ben's spring conference, Mrs. Margoles showed us Ben's final written product and explained that he had earned the highest mark, four out of four, which meant his paper exceeded third-grade expectations.

She handed the final draft to us, and we read, quickly skimming. Heavily penciled words filled the page from margin to margin and top to bottom. At the top of the page was the title "The Game," followed by a detailed play-by-play broadcast-style story describing a suspenseful soccer match. Complete with snappy goal-to-goal dialog, the reader was quickly drawn into the scene and eager to discover the outcome of the close game. The story concluded with a crowd-pleasing, grandstand-cheering ending for the final tie-breaking goal kick.

We congratulated Ben for the excellent job he did on the writing assignment. He shrugged it off and remained quiet, distant, and less than celebratory for the remainder of the conference.

"But Mom," Ben protested that night with the same vague anxiety that he had expressed in the past, "I'm not proud of myself. I still can't write. I can't." I winced at the thought that perhaps our own perfectionism had spilled over a bit too much onto him.

"Why?" I asked. "Tell me."

"Because I *had* to finish the story, I wrote whatever I could just to finish it." Ben looked up at me. "And it bothered me when you and Dad and Mrs. Margoles told me how good it was when I didn't even try."

After more discussion, it became clear to both Ben and me that his concept of writing went much deeper than that of the writing standards. He'd learned his first painful lesson about writing for school—that writing assignments could seem dull and meaningless, and the response could be just as uninspiring, not requiring real contemplation. I regretted that he had not come away with the knowledge that a writing assignment, or any other assignment for that matter, can be whatever you make of it, bad or good.

Sometimes giving 10% of your effort is all that is required to achieve what others consider a success, yet the outcome can still leave you personally dissatisfied. Ben was too inexperienced in life to understand that giving 10% to please others could actually be a useful strategy that would allow him to give the remaining 90% of his efforts to pursue something that really mattered to him. He would have been able to please others with a less-than-perfect performance and save his energy for the really important stuff. Judy Galbraith, author and publisher of books about gifted children's issues, couldn't have said it better: "Not everything worth doing is worth doing well."

A Little Research Expedition

Some decisions are important enough that they deserve a little research ahead of time. For Ben and Jillian, when it came to elementary school classroom placement, Brian and I felt that it was important to directly influence the decision on our children's behalf. In those years at the primary school, Mr. Swenson, whom we trusted, had final say over which teachers Ben and Jillian had, for which we were thankful. However, Ben would now be going to a new school, and we didn't know the principal or the usual process there. So we made it a priority to do a little research to find out who made those decisions and what the options were for parent input on classes and teachers.

In late May of Ben's third-grade year, Brian and I met with the principal of the Intermediate School, which would be Ben's school in the fall, and discussed Ben's history and our concerns. We also asked permission to visit a couple of teachers' classrooms. Mr. Marchetti supported the concept of more parental input when it came to classroom choice; in fact, he encouraged us to check out the teachers and get back to him.

We were particularly interested in learning about the shared classrooms of Mark Daly and Pete Wilson. We had heard about these teachers while chatting with other parents during soccer games last fall. We had talked particularly with another set of parents whose daughter was currently a fourth grader in Mr. Wilson's class.

Several unique characteristics attracted us to these classrooms. The two classes consisted of three mixed grades: fourth, fifth, and sixth. The entire school had had a variety of mixed

classes up to that year, until the logistics of it became more difficult than most teachers were willing to handle, due to the new
strictly implemented state standards. These two classrooms
were the only surviving pair to have mixed grades. We believed
that the opportunity for exposure to a variety of kids, levels of
thinking, and interactions would be a great fit for Ben. The
room was an open double-size classroom with a moveable
divider down the middle. The two teachers shared the space
and shared the students. A portion of time was spent in each
teacher's class, split three ways by grade levels for math, or
combined all together for science. Ben would have many
opportunities for interaction on varying levels, and he would
have two teachers to ask questions of, to confide in, or to just
plain joke around with. And since each teacher had a unique
style, Ben, as well as all of the other students, had double the
chance to learn from a teaching style that matched his own
unique learning style.

A few more subjective but no less significant aspects of this
mixed-grade classroom were that both teachers were second-
career teachers who had been team teaching for the last six
years. They had had successful careers prior to entering teaching
and were gifted in their own right. The unique backgrounds of
the teachers, combined with the environment and structure of
their classrooms, made their program sound like a perfect
opportunity for Ben.

Having learned from past experience that we couldn't rely
solely on other people's advice or opinions, I made an appointment for the following week to observe the classroom and check
it out myself.

Everything I had heard from talking with other parents at
soccer was reliable. However, visiting the teachers in person
during the school day helped me better understand who these
two unique individuals were, how they worked together, how
they implemented their teaching strategies, and how they shaped
the classroom culture. After spending only about 15 minutes

with each teacher, I liked what I saw, what I heard, and how the students interacted with each other. Most of all, I liked how the teachers interacted with the students. These two teachers were guides—not drill sergeants or hand holders. They encouraged students to think for themselves and take responsibility for their own learning.

In Mr. Daly's classroom, my first impression was one of chaos, but only because it was "choice time" and so many kids were doing so many different things. The activity and noise level was higher than one would find in most classrooms. Students were working on a variety of projects; some were drawing, some were finishing math assignments, and others were reviewing personal spelling lists together. I had to ask Mr. Daly what grades specific kids were in because there was no way of knowing by looking at how they socialized. Fourth graders mixed as freely with sixth graders as with each other. Expectations were clear, but students had a variety of ways and timelines in which to meet their academic and social goals.

In Mr. Wilson's classroom, activities were intentionally structured. The class sat in a large circle on the floor for the Spanish lesson while kids responded to questions from the teacher in an orderly and respectful manner. They were quiet, focused, and clearly understood the appropriate code for behavior at that moment. I should say that *most* of the kids understood; the few who didn't were firmly but respectfully reminded. What I saw in Mr. Daly's room contrasted with Mr. Wilson's room.

Mr. Daly seemed to have a higher tolerance for noise level and encouraged students to follow their own direction in how to complete tasks. In his room, students interacted more and, thus, at higher decibels. Mr. Wilson was more structured. He set the expectations clearly and encouraged students to figure things out themselves, but he didn't tolerate behavior that was outside of the defined limits. A student who could handle independent learning along with a higher level of social interaction might thrive in Mr. Daly's room, whereas a student who operated in a more linear fashion might do better with Mr. Wilson. Either way, these teachers and their students seemed to know when to pull in the reins and when to let loose.

After talking with the two teachers individually (for only a few minutes, because there was a constant stream of kids approaching and asking for help, opinions, and advice), each one told me why he loved teaching and how his way of teaching was so important for the kids to learn and grow into independent, happy people. I could see how having two teachers leading different parts of the day would benefit any child. There were more opportunities for meeting the needs of diverse learning styles. And with two teachers present, students had a choice about who they felt comfortable with when seeking help with nonacademic issues.

After reporting on my research to Brian later that day, we both agreed that if we had a choice, we would definitely advocate for Ben's fourth-grade placement into one of the mixed-grade classrooms.

Return to Sender, Classroom Unknown

Have you ever carefully mailed an important letter to an important person, only to find the envelope back in your mailbox three months later with "Return to sender—address unknown" stamped on the front? And then all the loose ends you thought you'd tied up in that letter suddenly came unraveled? That's what happened over the summer with a letter that Brian and I sent to the principal at Ben's new school requesting the next year's classroom placement. Except that our envelope was never returned. This was the letter.

> May 31,
>
> Dear Mr. Marchetti,
>
> Thank you for meeting with us earlier this month to discuss classroom placement options for our son, Ben, who is entering your school this fall as a fourth grader. I visited with Mr. Daly and Mr. Wilson in their classrooms and was able to see them in action, as well have them answer some of my questions.
>
> After discussing several options, my husband and I have decided to request that Ben be enrolled in the multi-age classroom of Mr. Wilson. We believe that, considering Ben's needs as a highly gifted learner and his personal learning style, he will best fit in Mr. Wilson's class.
>
> We have carefully considered how to advocate for our son in the past and consider this request as another important step in providing Ben with the best available environment in which to learn and generally just be the happy kid that he is.
>
> Thank you for considering our request. Please let us know Ben's classroom placement at your earliest convenience. If you have any questions, please do not hesitate to contact one of us.
>
> Sincerely,
> Wendy and Brian Skinner

I made the mistake of assuming that if we didn't hear from Mr. Marchetti, nothing was amiss. No news was good news. And with a busy summer full of camping, classes, and swimming at the recreation center, I didn't give Ben's placement at his new school another thought—that is, until Thursday, four days before school started.

As I pushed my shopping cart through the dairy section at our local grocery store. I nearly missed bumping into another cart.

"Oh, excuse me," I said. Then I recognized that the woman pushing the other cart was another parent from Ben's old school. "Carol!"

"Hi, Wendy! Sorry, it's my fault. I'm a maniac today," she apologized. "We just came back from vacation and I'm trying to do too many things at once before school starts. Say, do you know who Ben's teacher is yet?"

"No," I answered as I pushed my cart to the side to make more room for passersby.

"Matthew has Mrs. Keller," Carol said. "I checked the postings."

"They're up at the school?" I asked, puzzled.

"Yes, just today—Oh, gosh! I've got to get going," Carol said as she glanced at her watch. "I've got to pick the kids up in 10 minutes."

Carol and I said our goodbyes, and I finished my shopping. I felt a tinge of excitement when she said that class lists were posted at the school. I'd heard by word of mouth that this was a tradition, but I'd never gotten any formal notice. I'd stop by and check the lists on my way home.

On my way to the school, I thought, if I hadn't seen Carol, I wouldn't have known that the lists were up. "That seems pretty strange, even irresponsible," I thought to myself, "not to notify parents in writing."

I walked up the sidewalk to the front entrance of the new school. From the outside, I could see more than a dozen white sheets of paper taped to the front foyer's windows. Several parents chatted in front of the windows as they shuffled back and forth, bending closer and squatting to read the typed lists. Donna, a friend of mine with a daughter in Ben's grade, was there.

"Hi, Donna. Checking class lists, I see." My eyes began scanning Mr. Wilson's class list.

"Oh, hi," Donna replied. She took off her sunglasses and waved them in the air. "Maybe I could read the lists better without these on," she laughed. "Have you gotten all your school supplies yet for Ben? That last supply list is different from the one they gave us in the spring."

"Supply list?" I asked. "I never got one."

"Oh, you know; it was in the packet that came in the mail last week." she said matter-of-factly. "Oh! Here she is." Donna pointed to a sheet at the bottom of the window. "Marissa's in Miss Reilly's class. And here's Ben," Donna called, pointing to another sheet next to Miss Reilly's class list. "Mrs. Meyers. He's in Mrs. Meyer's class."

Mrs. *Who?* I thought. Who is Mrs. Meyers? What happened to Mr. Wilson?

My eyes caught sight of a sheet above Mrs. Meyer's list with MR. WILSON typed across the top in capital letters. Maybe Donna had read wrong. I read and reread the list to no avail. Ben's name was missing from Mr. Wilson's list, and sure enough, there it was on the list of students in Mrs. Meyer's class. My heart dropped into my stomach with disappointment.

"See you later, Donna," I said with a sinking feeling. "I've got groceries in the van."

I turned the key in the ignition and pondered the situation, going over the facts in my mind. We never received a supply list at the end of last year. We didn't receive a school information packet last week. And Ben was *not* in Mr. Wilson's class, as we had requested. What did all this mean?

After a little more thought, I realized that we had never completed the usual district-wide year-end parent input form regarding classroom placement for the following school year. And we had never received a route schedule with a bus assignment from the bus company.

Why hadn't it dawned on me earlier in the summer that we had received no communication regarding Ben's enrollment? What was wrong with me? What had I been waiting for? I thought, "Wouldn't you know, the one time you assume things will take care of themselves, it's Murphy's Law all over again." I chided myself in the van as I pulled away from the school, "The one time you weren't worried, you should have been."

I drove straight home, brought the groceries into the house, and put away the freezer and refrigerator items. The rest could wait while I made a phone call.

I called the school office. The secretary told me I wasn't the first parent to call and that some of the packets had been lost in the mail. She confirmed that the packets mailed in June had indeed contained the standard parent input form regarding classroom placement. Although Ben was on record for Mrs. Meyer's class, she apologized for us not receiving any of the parent mailings.

When I asked her about our letter to Mr. Marchetti, she could find no record of it. She then informed me of Mr. Marchetti's unexpected retirement over the summer, which may have had something to do with our missing letter. When we'd met with Mr. Marchetti and written the letter, Brian and I were totally unaware of any retirement plans. What happened to our letter? Had it met its demise in the paper shredder by mistake, or had it simply vaporized in the summer heat? Obviously, our personal written communication to Mr. Marchetti had made no difference whatsoever when it came to ensuring Ben's placement with the teacher we wanted him to have.

My next call was to the bus company. They had no record of Ben from the school's master list. When I explained the situation, they said they'd check with the school and take care of it. Somehow Ben had made it to an individual class list but was absent from the master list, and as a result, we had missed all communication sent out from the school.

Next, I got in touch with Tina Jansen from Ben's former school, as well as the new gifted teacher and the secretary at the new Intermediate School. After full discussions of the circumstances, both gifted teachers agreed that Ben needed to be in Mr. Wilson's mixed-grade classroom. "I'll take care of it, Wendy,"

Tina Jansen assured me. "Don't worry. I'll call you when we have it settled."

By the end of the morning, as the last cereal box was put up on the shelf, Tina called back. She confirmed that Ben was now in Mr. Wilson's class, that the bus company now had Ben on their list, and that all the appropriate materials would be mailed out to us immediately. I thanked her profusely. I was very grateful that she knew us and that she and the other gifted teacher were able to use their expertise, knowledge, experience, and influence to advocate for Ben at such a critical point.

With a sigh of relief, I called Brian. "I just had a two-hour adrenaline rush," I joked.

When he heard the story, Brian said, "I'm so glad you were able to just take it by the horns and take care of it." Then he paused and said, "Thank you, really."

I learned a huge lesson that Thursday morning. I learned to ask, then to confirm, and sometimes to reconfirm. No news does *not* always mean good news.

A Love Affair with Backgammon

"Snacks out and ready?"

"Check!"

"Four tables set up with chairs?"

"Check!"

"Game instruction diagram at each table?"

"Check!"

"It's almost 1:00. Everyone should be arriving any minute." I wiped the crumbs and smudges off the kitchen counter and took a long, deep breath. Our house was about to be invaded by nearly a dozen fourth and fifth graders for two hours. Their mission? To be the winner in Ben's backgammon tournament.

The previous Saturday, the word "backgammon" wasn't even in Ben's vocabulary. Then Wednesday came, and backgammon was all he could talk about.

"Mom," Ben shouted as he came into the house through the back door that day. "Mom, I want to have a backgammon tournament. I'm *going* to have a backgammon tournament." He peeled his backpack from his body and tossed it on the counter. "How about Saturday?"

"No 'hello'? No kiss for your mother?" I asked with my hands on my hips.

"Sorry, Mom." Ben squeezed his arms around me, and as I leaned down, he lightly kissed me. "So how about Saturday?"

"How about Sunday?" I countered. "But tell me, what's this all about?"

Mr. Wilson had taught the class how to play backgammon the day before, and now the whole class was crazy about the game. By dinnertime, Ben had commandeered our old backgammon board from the basement and had challenged everyone in the family to a game. We played every day after that. I hadn't played for so long that I had to rely on Ben to teach me the rules. Each day for the next week, when Ben came home from school, he felt compelled to inform me of additional rules he'd missed or misunderstood. By Sunday's tournament, he thought he had enough hours of backgammon under his belt to have a good chance at winning.

Of the dozen kids invited, four girls and five boys showed up to eat popcorn, drink lemonade, and play backgammon for two hours. Three tables held competing pairs; we had two games in the dining room, one game on the front porch coffee table and another game in the living room. Although Jillian was not included in the official four female competitors, she participated fully in the conversation and laughter, especially with the older girls. Considering how many children were confined to just two rooms in our house, it was surprisingly quiet. The boys and girls had nothing on their minds but victory.

After an hour, it became apparent that two hours would not give each competitor enough time to play every other competitor. When the time was up and the first parents began to arrive,

Ben had to declare three winners: Richelle, Isaac, and himself. None of these "winners" had yet played each other, however, so it truly was a three-way tie.

"Thank you so much for having Isaac over," one mother said as she picked up her son. "It's all he could talk about for days."

"Don't thank me. Thank Ben," I answered. "It was all his idea. I just provided the refreshments."

It was true. Ben had organized and coordinated the whole thing. He'd determined the guest list, called all the guests within the first 10 minutes of hatching the plan, and made sure his young friends all brought backgammon games of their own to share. With a little help from me, we scanned and printed out game instructional diagrams (to be sure everyone got off to a proper start) and organized a tournament chart.

It dawned on me later that day that the backgammon party was a great example of how far Ben had come in adjusting to his acceleration in school—not only academically, but socially. He showed all the confidence and enthusiasm for hosting the backgammon event that I could have ever dreamed of. But perhaps more importantly, he had shared his interest and enthusiasm for a new skill with other like-minded kids, and together they simply had a great time.

Chapter 7

Kindergarten or First?

It seems to me that parents tend to focus their memories (and their cameras) most often on their firstborn child. I am no different; Ben made the greatest mark on my memory, blazing his path through my memory neurons with novelty and surprises. But Jillian, although she was second born, was certainly equally worthy of special notice. With the added complexities that come with raising two children, I had to make a concerted effort to take the memories of Jillian from my brain and put them down on paper.

While Ben settled into first grade at his new public school and made rapid progress, Jillian continued in her second year at preschool. Her teacher often commented that she seemed more like a kindergartner than a preschooler. She was coordinated, possessed a willowy frame, and her intelligence and social skills were apparent to many adults. She always preferred playing with the older children or the creatively active boys instead of her female age mates, who regularly gravitated toward dress-up or the playhouse area. It was not uncommon for children and adults alike to assume that Jillian was a year older than she was.

We had not considered an early start in kindergarten for Jillian because of her late August birthday. She was already younger than some of the children in her current preschool class. Besides, she and I had a lot of exploration still to do at home, where we had the luxury of unscheduled open days. But with the start of school and kindergarten fast approaching in the fall, Brian and I suddenly realized that although Jillian was still young, she would have her own set of unique problems in school, and perhaps specifically with kindergarten placement. Having learned from our experiences with Ben, we took a proactive position to plan ahead with Jillian instead of waiting for problems to arise.

In July, I called the same psychologist who had tested Ben and explained Jillian's situation. Although it is sometimes difficult to test children as young as four years and 11 months, the psychologist tested Jillian with the Stanford-Binet, L-M, the Woodcock-Johnson Achievement Tests, and in addition, the *Vineland Adaptive Behavior Scales*, which measure nonacademic adaptive skills. Jillian's scores showed that she had a mental age of eight years and eight months. She scored in the highly gifted range, like her brother. Her Woodcock-Johnson score showed an early kindergarten level in reading and an early first-grade level for math. The Vineland test indicated that her adaptive skills of self-care, socialization, and independence were comparable to an average nine-year-old.

In many ways, Jillian scored uncannily like her brother. Dr. Mullen noted that some research shows that siblings will likely test within five to 10 points of each other on an IQ test. Between the three of us—Dr. Mullen, Brian, and me—we agreed that the school should look at the possibility of accelerating Jillian either immediately to first grade or of skipping a grade in the future.

When I called Mr. Swenson, the principal, he said that his standard policy was to give a child a full month for observation in kindergarten before the she could be considered for a skip to first grade. We set up a meeting with Mr. Swenson, Jillian's kindergarten teacher Mrs. Murphy, and Mrs. Jansen, the gifted teacher, to discuss possibilities.

Before the meeting, Mrs. Jansen administered a test called the *Gesell Developmental Schedules* for Jillian. After researching the Gesell test, I found that it was initially used to identify boys who were not developmentally ready for kindergarten. It reportedly had other applications, but it was not in any way an intellectual test. I asked Dr. Mullen about this test, and he said that he hadn't heard of it being used very often in recent years. He questioned the validity of such a test being used for identifying developmental maturity in a gifted child, much less determining whether or not a child should be accelerated.[13]

I made my own mental preparations before the school meeting. I was concerned with two issues in particular. I wanted neither Jillian's chronological age nor her gender to distract from meeting her overall needs. Some of my concern undoubtedly came from my own experiences with school and a lack of challenge in my early years.

Because I, too, had an August birthday, my parents didn't feel a need to put me into kindergarten a year early. However, throughout most of my school years, in spite of my young age, I rarely had to work to make good grades, and most academic situations required only a minimal amount effort from me.

The one exception to this was my childhood aversion to reading, which began in the third grade. I was moved from the top reading group to the middle and began having difficulty reading with accuracy. I got glasses, which I wore only for that year before realizing they didn't really make a difference. Looking back at it now, I wonder whether, if I were in elementary school today, I might have been diagnosed with some sort of reading disability. But in spite of my early difficulty with reading, I more than compensated, and I managed to score at eleventh-grade reading level in the sixth grade.

When I finally had the opportunity in high school to challenge myself with various Advanced Placement classes and upper-level math classes, I chose the easier classes instead. The extra reading requirements of the advanced classes intimidated me, and the math courses seemed far too great a challenge. Grades were important to me. I didn't want to attempt anything that I might fail or do poorly at. I avoided classes that required putting my nose to a book for extended periods of time, which included Advanced Placement history and English. And although I was a B+ to A- math student up through geometry and algebra II, I caved in on trigonometry and decided that I just didn't have the brain for it. As my teachers and parents said at the time, I didn't apply myself. I never gave myself the opportunity to really work hard at something. I don't remember asking others to help me, nor do I remember being offered any extra help from teachers or my parents.

Later I realized that because I never needed to develop study skills or the grit determination to succeed in difficult courses, the high school classes that were more challenging became roadblocks to further developing my full academic potential. I remember examining a career chart hanging prominently on a wall in the math department listing each math class required for different occupations. I was quite disappointed to see that to pursue any of the life science careers that interested me, I would have to take advanced math well beyond algebra II and would even have to take calculus at some point. It was a mental and emotional turning point for me—one which I truly regret. By not signing up for trigonometry or any math beyond geometry, I thereby closed the door and gave up all hope of pursuing any of the high-paying fields of study involving science, engineering, medicine, and even architecture. All required higher math.

I was determined that things would be different for Jillian. I wanted her to be challenged right off the bat, and to continue to be challenged at school. I wanted her to develop the tenacity and skill to tackle difficult problems that would result in greater personal and tangible rewards.

I read *Reviving Ophelia* by Mary Pipher, Ph.D, a book about the many challenges faced by teenage girls, and *Smart Girls: A New Psychology of Girls, Women, and Giftedness* by

Barbara A. Kerr, Ph.D., about the societal dangers and institutionalized biases working against girls in school. I also read numerous articles and heard speakers address these same issues.

In spite of Jillian's strong personality, I feared that she might fall into the submissive, quiet, don't-attract-too-much-attention mentality described in these books that is all too often reinforced by authority figures, including teachers. According to many experts, this kind of passive mentality is a factor that can thwart the academic development of prepubescent and adolescent girls.

I did not want Jillian to be overlooked because of her gender or because of her obedience and respect for authority. She had a quiet way of handling conflict outside of the home. If something was not going well for her at school, she was more likely to hold her frustration in rather than play the role of the proverbial squeaky wheel. I would have to do the squeaking for her, for now. Perhaps I was projecting too many of my own fears into Jillian's current situation, but I sincerely wanted to make the best decisions regarding her education every step of the way.

Before Brian and I attended the meeting regarding early entrance to first grade, we discussed the possible outcomes. Brian had a more open mind than I, possibly because he had not immersed himself in all the reading and discussions about advocating for gifted children. I had drawn up my personal agenda, but Brian did not have a particular agenda. As we bounced our thoughts and ideas around that evening, it seemed that Brian agreed with me no matter how my position fluctuated. As his primary source of information and opinion, I possessed a strong influence over what information he was exposed to.

On the one hand, I resented his disinterest in reading up on gifted issues himself. However, on the other hand, I understood that his time was rigidly structured each day, whereas mine was quite flexible, and I actually enjoyed my role as researcher and informer on education issues. It seemed an efficient way to organize our parenting partnership. Brian usually trusted my

judgment when it came to the children's education. He appreciated the initiative I took in the search for information and
understanding about gifted children.

At noon on a sunny October day, five of us—Mr. Swenson,
Mrs. Murphy, Mrs. Jansen, Brian, and I—gathered at a table in
Jillian's kindergarten room. At the beginning of the meeting,
Mr. Swenson and his staff made it clear that they would support
whatever decision we made. Given the intellectual and academic information they had gathered, they thought that Jillian
could go either way; she could stay in kindergarten or go on to
first grade. Mrs. Murphy said she liked Jillian very much, and
although she would support our decision, she would sorely miss
having the chance to work with Jillian for the year if she were
accelerated to first grade. But Mrs. Murphy also expressed some
concern.

"When my class of kindergartners finished last year, they were
really ready for first grade. Their level of readiness was far beyond
what I perceive Jillian's to be at this time," she said. I mentally
countered, "True. However, that doesn't mean that Jillian couldn't
quickly catch up and adapt, given the opportunity."

Mrs. Jansen reported that according to the Gesell test, Jillian
was at a typical kindergarten level of general development.

Brian and I left the meeting without making a decision. We
thanked everyone for their efforts and concerns and told them
that we would let Mrs. Murphy know by the next day what we
decided. We walked out the school's front doors hand-in-hand.

"So? What do you think?" I asked Brian in as neutral a tone
as possible. I didn't want to project my feelings onto him before
he had a chance to express himself.

Without hesitation, he said, "I want Jillian to stay in kindergarten. I feel so strongly about this. She *needs* to stay where she
is. We can't push her, Wendy."

Upon hearing Brian's first words, the pent-up tension from
the past few days broke inside me. This was not what I wanted
to hear. But Brian had rarely spoken with such firmness and

conviction on anything like this before, and the certainty in his voice deflected my urge to challenge. Did he think I was pushing her? Was he concerned about the teacher comment that children who finished kindergarten with her were at a higher level than Jillian at present?

I conceded without eye contact, "Yes. You're right. Better to have her stay in kindergarten with Mrs. Murphy than to move her to first grade and have it be a mistake. There's time in the future for Jillian to move ahead. Just not now...."

We gave each other a quick kiss goodbye before parting, but the moment I turned my back, tears began pouring out of my eyes. I was crushed. My hopes for giving Jillian the upper hand were abruptly abandoned. However, I could not ignore the reality that the best decision was not solely *my* decision, but my husband's as well.

In previous conversations, Brian and I had agreed that if we kept Jillian in kindergarten, she could always accelerate in the future. However, if it *didn't* work out after moving her to first grade, we were concerned that either forcing her to stay or returning to kindergarten would be painful.[14]

Brian's position was not negotiable, and mine was. If keeping Jillian in kindergarten was not the best choice, it could be easily remedied by moving her to first grade. Though disappointed, I could accept his position because I knew it could always be re-evaluated and changed. Going to first grade would be a step forward with no looking back, and Brian could not accept the fact that if we were wrong, going back to kindergarten would not be a choice. His position was safer and more conservative, while mine was risky. His position was based on sound, defendable reasoning, while mine, admittedly, weighed more heavily on emotion and gut feelings. I knew I needed to yield to his reasoning because I had to admit that it did make more sense for Jillian. More importantly, I knew that yielding to Brian's conviction was an important demonstration to him that I respected his position as an equal parenting partner. Up to this point, I had taken the lead with Ben and Jillian's education, pressed my agenda tirelessly with Brian, and assumed a righteous position in our roles as guardians. It was time to share more of the power and listen more to other options. Brian deserved a stronger voice in our decisions.

Over the next few days, I gradually let go of my emotional attachments to accelerating Jillian to first grade. I became comfortable with her being in kindergarten. However, my reasons for keeping her there were not necessarily the same reasons for which Mr. Swenson, Mrs. Murphy, and Mrs. Jansen wanted to keep her there. I felt that Jillian *was* capable of thriving in first grade, and I believed that she was developmentally *ready* for first grade. But looking at the bigger picture, I added up all of the positive factors that would, and ultimately did, serve Jillian well over the next year or two. One positive reason to keep Jillian in kindergarten was the opportunity to have Mrs. Murphy for a teacher.

Over the short time that I'd known Mrs. Murphy, I had formed the opinion that she was a superb match for our Jillian. At our very first meeting, the day before kindergarten began, Mrs. Murphy connected with Jillian immediately in a firm, authoritative, yet respectful way. Within 10 minutes, she had Jillian's reading and writing ability and level pegged. I'd never seen a teacher assess and set the tone in so little time as Mrs. Murphy did. I was a total bystander as Brian and I watched her hand Jillian a lined sheet of paper and a pencil.

"Write 'I love Taft School,' on this paper, Jillian," Mrs. Murphy commanded while making direct eye contact. Jillian obeyed and proceeded to do her best in letter formation and phonic spelling. I had never seen Jillian sit down and actually write an entire dictated sentence like this before.

"Now," Mrs. Murphy continued, "read these words the best you can." Mrs. Murphy held up, one at a time, a dozen or so sight words, and Jillian proceeded to respond, reading about three or four of them, like "dog," "cat," "I," and other very simple words. Mrs. Murphy then asked Jillian to count as far as she could. I could sense the teacher's intense engagement, like a detective looking for clues during an interrogation, as she listened and watched my daughter's every word and move.

I later learned while volunteering in her classroom that Mrs. Murphy was a very organized teacher who packed a lot into a short kindergarten morning. In addition to her efficiency, she was an expert storyteller. When she told the class all about her travels in China, Jillian soaked in the rich vocabulary and cultural concepts and responded enthusiastically. Additionally, Mrs. Murphy was not shy about offering parenting advice or letting me know about educational opportunities available to Jillian. I took her advice occasionally and appreciated her enthusiasm and concern for Jillian's development. She was a strong teacher who challenged both of us that year.

Another positive aspect of keeping Jillian in kindergarten was the smaller class size. For an entire year, Jillian benefited from being in a class of only 17 students, when most classes were 25 or more. Within the small class, Mrs. Murphy used her teacher's aide, Mrs. Rodriguez, to lead a reading group of three to four children, which included Jillian. Smaller class sizes were an advantage as long as Jillian was challenged in kindergarten and then again in first grade. They meant that the teacher could give more attention not only to Jillian's needs, but to every other child's needs as well. This created a more focused classroom, more teacher-to-pupil time, and less time spent on discipline or classroom management issues.

Another advantage to keeping Jillian in kindergarten was that she had a full year of home school-like experiences. She and I had an entire afternoon every day to do things together. We were free to work on projects, read, go to the library, and go on outings. Jillian began Suzuki violin lessons and could take advantage of an open afternoon to practice.

Perhaps the greatest advantage to keeping Jillian in kindergarten, however, was that Brian, the school staff, and I could always re-evaluate the possibility of accelerating her at a later date. Our years of helping Ben through the academic maze provided us with experience, some perspective, and a proactive attitude. Armed with Jillian's intellectual and psychological test results, and with positive relationships with school staff, we were confident that we would be able to effectively advocate for our daughter as she progressed through school.

Dissecting with Dr. Jillian

Gifted children sometimes have many interests and seem to follow them by some sort of instinct. I've learned to trust my children's instincts and to accommodate their interests. I used to hesitate, wondering if my effort, time, and money would see a return if invested in the interest "du jour," but I no longer question the motivation. I believe that a variety of investigative experiences in childhood help build a whole child and, eventually, a whole and happy adult. Whether the experiences are object-, place-, or person-centered, whether they last for a day, a week, a month, a year, or eventually develop into a lifelong fulfilling occupation, they add a layer of depth to the child, preadolescent, adolescent, and ultimately the mature person that the child is becoming.

Gifted kids often pursue unusual interests and activities. For example, Ben chose to learn to play accordion. Brian and I didn't play the accordion. None of his friends played the accordion. Fortunately for our family, Brian's aunt and his deceased grandfather did play it, so we inherited two old family accordions as gifts when Ben's relatives learned of his interest.

At a young age, Jillian had a biologist's fascination for all things living. When her interest peaked in anatomy and physiology, we supported her interest and enthusiasm before it faded or morphed into some other fascination.

In the spring of Jillian's kindergarten year, I found evidence of a small but pesky intruder in my greenhouse. After discovering my tiny seedlings decapitated, pulled up at the roots, or just plain dug out of their small pots, I knew I'd have to resort to a defensive strategy—mousetraps. It only took one night and one trap to catch the vandal, but to my regret, the varmint was not a mouse but a chipmunk. To make things worse, the trap was too small and had only given the chipmunk a severe thump on the head. The poor thing. It was obviously confused as it crawled in an endless tight circle. I was afraid it would not survive the night.

I found a pair of leather work gloves and grabbed a small, old, plastic ice cream pail. Upon returning to the greenhouse, I found the chipmunk in its futile efforts to escape, still hopelessly traveling in circles. I gently scooped up the little furball and brought it to the garage, put some dry grass clippings and leaves in the pail, and wedged it in the woodpile with an old t-shirt rag laid over the top to keep the spring chill out. I let it rest protected overnight in the cozy pail to give it the best chance for recovery.

When Jillian came home from kindergarten, she wanted to see the chipmunk—not from idle curiosity, but because over the school year, her interest in the internal activities of humans and animals had increased. She had already made numerous requests to dissect a real animal. If the chipmunk survived, I would return it to its foraging ways, though away from my plants. If the chipmunk died, its body would be put to good use. Jillian would have the specimen she'd been asking for.

That evening, while still confined to the security of the plastic pale, the chipmunk had tucked itself into a tight round ball with its tail wrapped up around its head. The tiny chest raised and lowered steadily as it slept. In the early morning, when Jillian and I checked the chipmunk on our way to meet the kindergarten bus, its body hadn't moved the slightest since we'd last checked on it the night before. However, its chest had ceased its steady rhythm, and it lay still.

"Oh, Mom," Jillian sighed as she peeked under the t-shirt rag at the tiny corpse. "Poor little chipmunk."

"We tried our best," I said, "but I'm afraid it just wasn't going to make it."

"So Mom," Jillian's voice lifted from its mournful tone to one of guarded optimism. "Does this mean we can dissect it now?"

Later that morning after Jillian returned from kindergarten, I pulled the plastic-wrapped chipmunk's body from the refrigerator and set it in a large glass pie pan. Jillian and I draped ourselves in full aprons and pulled latex gloves onto our hands. We gathered the necessary tools: tweezers, knife, paper towels, and plastic safety goggles. I did most of the actual slicing according to Jillian's direction.

"Mom, Mom! I want to see the heart and the lungs and its stomach. Everything. I want to see *everything*," Jillian said with great excitement, her eyes glued to the chipmunk's body. "And the brain, too!"

With the hide of the chipmunk peeled away from its belly and ribs, we were able to collect many specimens.

"Look! Look! I see a blood vessel. It's a tube!"

"That's the aorta, the main artery that takes fresh, oxygenated blood away from the heart...."

"Oooh! That's a lung?"

"Yes, white and spongy, see? It's turning pinker as we look at it."

"I know why. That's because the blood is exposed to the oxygen in the air...look! That kidney looks just like a little jelly bean!"

The specimens occupied us for several hours. By the end of the afternoon, Jillian had a tiny glass contact lens vial filled with a kidney, a lung, a heart, and a sample of brain tissue—all soaking in alcohol.

The next day at school "Dr. Jillian" visited each of the morning kindergarten classes carrying the small transparent vial filled with miniature internal organs for everyone to see. Fortunately, her teacher shared Jillian's enthusiasm for anatomy and physiology (her son was in medical school, an aspiring surgeon). I greatly appreciated the way all of the teachers welcomed the impromptu science samples and the discussion they inspired—with respect and sensitively. There were 16 other curious kindergartners in Jillian's class, as well as those in the other kindergarten classes. And that little vial occupied a valued spot on top of Jillian's dresser for nearly three years.

The chipmunk's remains did not sit alone for long. Later that summer, Jillian found a hatchling painted turtle on the side of the street. Because it had been unable to climb over the curb to the coolness of the grass, it had succumbed to fatal consequences from the heat collecting on the dark asphalt of the street. Jillian placed the quarter-size reptile in a small jam jar, where it rested peacefully at the bottom of its alcohol bath.

In the winter of first grade, we discovered a freshly frozen blue jay, its wings splayed on top of the cold snow with a wobbly broken neck. It was a collision casualty resulting from the daily ruckus surrounding a neighbor's freshly filled birdfeeder. This time, Jillian used a real dissecting kit that she'd received as a Christmas present, purchased from a bioengineering supply store and which included a wax tray, pins, scalpel, etc. The poor bird's stomach was nearly bursting with so much birdseed that we mistook it at first for a large egg. On this occasion, Jillian decided not to keep the internal organs and instead chose the two flexing, grasping, dinosaur-like feet. Now she had chipmunk organs, a sleeping baby turtle, and a blue jay's feet. Not what you might find in a university research lab, but not a bad start for a six-year-old possible future biologist.

Fairness and Tradition

That July, before Jillian began first grade, it was a day like so many others in Minnesota: temperatures in the 90s, humid, and hazy. To keep cool, Ben wore nothing but underwear and shorts to play around the house. No one gave it a second thought. Dress for the weather. Parka, snow pants, hat, gloves, scarves, and boots for winter. Shorts and bare feet for summer.

For practical purposes, Jillian adopted this attire as well. Were it not for her long golden brown hair brushing her shoulder blades, the two of them could easily have passed for twins in their androgynous five- and eight-year-old forms—two wiry, slender, athletic bodies wearing nothing but blue knit shorts.

"I'm taking Ginger out for a walk," I called from the back door, leash in hand. Our golden retriever, ears up, mouth open and panting, was poised, ready to go. "Who wants to go with me?"

"I will, I will," Jillian shouted and came running from the living room.

"Great." I smiled. "Find a shirt and put some shoes on."

"I don't need a shirt." Jillian grabbed her sandals.

"Yes, you do."

"No," Jillian sat down on the top step. "I don't. It's hot, and I'm just fine without a shirt."

"Please put a shirt on," I said more firmly. "We can talk about it on our walk."

Jillian left with a huff and reappeared a few minutes later wearing a bright yellow t-shirt.

What I'd hoped would be a relaxing walk through the park and neighborhood streets turned into a heated debate on the merits of social conformation and Western cultural gender roles.

"*Why* do I have to wear a shirt?" Jillian threw up her hands and sighed. "Ben doesn't have to wear a shirt, so why do I?"

"Because in our country, in our culture, if you're a girl, you are expected to wear a shirt," I explained. "It's all right to go without a shirt inside our house, with our own family, but when you leave the house, you need a shirt."

"But…"

"Wait, I'm not finished." I unleashed Ginger to run in the park. "And this is because in our culture, women *and* girls are expected to cover their tops when they go out in public."

"But why? *Why*? It isn't fair that just because I'm a girl I have to wear a shirt and Ben doesn't."

"It isn't," I agreed. "It isn't fair, I know. That's just the way it is." I added one more aspect that I thought might clarify the issue, "Jillian, it also has to do with modesty and"

"What do you mean?" Jillian interrupted.

"Modesty," I repeated and paused. I realized that this was going to get into other areas I might not be prepared for. Ginger treed a squirrel and was now trotting along the edge of the woods. "Remember what I said about how women and girls are expected to cover their chests?" And this was the part that I found so difficult to explain, because it was more complicated than anything I could describe to a six-year-old. "They cover their chests so as not to show off the private parts of their bodies."

"But Mom," Jillian's anger transformed briefly but distinctly into a plea like that of a child falsely accused of lying. "I am *not* showing off my body. I'm just *hot*." The anger returned. "It's not *fair!*"

I called Ginger over and reattached the leash to her collar. Jillian and I continued our discussion as we left the park. She repeated her concerns over and over, absolutely refusing to accept the illogical (to her) argument I presented that supported cultural gender discrimination.

"Why?" Jillian repeated to herself for the next 15 minutes. "Why? Just because I'm a girl? It's just not fair!" It was as if asking these questions over and over would somehow change the unforgiving cultural reality. Her last words of protest and pleas for fairness flew from her lips by the end of the walk. By the time we reached our front steps, the healing of walking and talking seemed to have soothed her enough to let her think about other things.

I wondered what impact this discussion would have on Jillian in the future. Surely other girls have questioned wearing a shirt on a hot day, but Jillian's dispute was an indication to me that she was keenly aware of examining her role in the world and how she would play that role. I desperately hoped that she would keep her strong sense of justice and fairness and her questioning spirit as she grew older.[15]

A Multidimensional Discussion

As a child, I remember intriguing discussions with my older brother, Michael, who has since become a research physicist. When he was about 10 or 12, I remember that he spoke of science fiction and philosophical topics such as the beginnings and limits of the universe, black holes, time travel, and paradoxes. I was reminded of these mind-stretching dreamy ideas one afternoon when I overheard Ben, eight and a half, and Jillian, who'd just turned six a few days before, develop their own theories regarding the nature of one-, two-, and three-dimensional objects.

Ben may have picked up some of these ideas from a favorite science show on television. But also, in his mixed-grade classroom of fourth through sixth graders, they were using a drawing program called *Draw Squad*, which taught three-dimensional drawing techniques such as perspective and shading.

"You're three-dimensional, Jillian," Ben declared. "I'm three-dimensional, and this Lego block is 3-D." Ben held a red Lego brick up as if to examine it for the first time. The two of them sat in the middle of a sea of Legos on the carpeted floor of the upstairs common area. A partially completed Lego house and Lego vehicle were abruptly neglected for the moment.

"Mom is 3-D, too," Jillian said, pointing to me while I tapped at the computer keys in the corner. Jillian bounced to her feet and pulled out a sheet of paper from my desk. "Ben," she said as she waved the sheet a foot from his face, "*this* is two dimensional. It's flat. 2-D."

I couldn't resist interjecting, "It's only the image that's 2-D, Jillian. Remember, the paper has a thickness on its side. Look," I said, pointing to the shelves beside me. "Look! You can really see how paper does have a thickness when it's all stacked up."

"Okay, yeah," Ben said. "Its image is 2-D. So Jillian," Ben paused for emphasis, then asked, "what is *one* dimension?"

Jillian crossed her legs and, resting her right elbow on the carpet, set her chin in the palm of her hand. She fell silent and still. Ben began adding black narrow bricks to the perimeter of his Lego truck's bed.

"Yeah," Ben spoke softly almost to himself. "One dimension. Can't be thick. Can't be wide. Can't be tall." Then louder, directly to his silent sister, "What *can* a one-dimensional object be?"

Jillian didn't appear to be listening, but her brain was fully engaged.

"Sound?" Ben asked.

"Light," Jillian said as she looked up with a sparkle of discovery in her voice.

Both children pondered their new ideas about one dimension. Suddenly, Jillian broke her stillness, her body abruptly expanding like a baking soda and vinegar concoction. Arms out, eyes wide open with her torso leaning forward toward Ben in her moment of revelation, she exclaimed, "A one-dimensional object is like when you try to see a paper hologram from the side!"

First Grade

First grade was filled with happy events and activities for Jillian. I think she felt more mature now that she attended school all day, ate lunch in the cafeteria, and rode the bus with the big kids. Because of our previous communication with Jillian's teacher and the principal, we were satisfied that the new teacher was a good fit for Jillian's needs.

Mrs. Tellmann, a confident and seasoned teacher, provided a rich variety of experiences for students in her class, had a consistent and firm classroom management style, and was a wonderful hugger (high on my daughter's priority list). It only took a week into the school year for me to feel confident that Jillian was in the right place at the right time. Not only did she have a terrific kindergarten year, but I could see that this first-grade year would not be wasted either.

Of course, there were ups and downs for Jillian, but for the most part, it was an even-keeled year. Some of the major highlights for her were that: (1) she belonged to Mrs. Tellmann's book club (a group of about seven advanced readers who met twice a week for reading and discussions), (2) she dressed up as The Lady of Wild Things for Halloween (her favorite character from *The Arcadians*, by Lloyd Alexander), (3) she found a kindred spirit and became best friends with a classmate named Tenesha, (4) she read all the books in *The Magic Treehouse* series by Mary Pope Osborne, and (5) she participated in her first year of the gifted program in school.

Although first grade was full and rewarding most of the time, Jillian often reported that she didn't like math because it was boring. In general, she was happy with her classmates and loved her teacher, but academically, I could tell she was on the edge of that fine line between contentedness and lack of challenge. Her rate of learning was so rapid that she would catch on to things very quickly, master the concept of the lesson, and want to be done with it. She had little patience for reviewing what she already knew. Her complaints were an accurate barometer for the amount of appropriately challenging work in which she was or was not engaged. And the complaints gradually increased as the year progressed like an undercurrent in a stream—gaining enough speed to be of concern, but not so visible on the surface as to cause alarm.

During Jillian's first-grade year, Brian and I were more relaxed. Although Jillian was walking on that edge of discontent, Mrs. Tellmann provided her with just enough stimulation to keep her from slipping off—for now. However, I couldn't see the next year, second grade, as a status quo year. By the end of first grade, Jillian was pushing the envelope with her reading skills (by her seventh birthday at the end of the summer, she'd read all of the C.S. Lewis *Narnia* series books), her insatiable desire for knowledge, and her fascination with more sophisticated scientific concepts. If we added three more months of development over the summer, she was bound to need more challenge than she would find in an average second-grade class.

Growing Up Bigger

A birthday is special to a child after weeks of anticipation, and Jillian was no exception. There is so much to look forward to: thoughtful gifts, birthday cake with candles, and special hugs and kisses all day long. A year older. Early in August, just before Jillian turned seven, she gave daily announcements proclaiming the number of days until her birthday and the number of days until the first day of school in September as a second grader.

The night of her birthday, after second and third helpings of leftover angel food birthday cake and subsequent tooth brushing, Jillian retreated especially contentedly to her bedroom. "I'll be up to kiss you goodnight soon, honey!" I called up the stairs after her.

I was about to knock on her door before entering when I noticed that, smack dab in the center of the door, at about eye level for a particular seven-year-old, was taped a freshly made sign. Carefully written in heavy dark marker were the words "I'm 7!" The "7" appeared 20 times the size of the "I'm" and stood boldly alone in the center of the sheet. Written below the gigantic "7" in small letters were the words "DO <u>NOT</u> ENTER!"

The sign seemed to not only mark the event of having grown another year older, but it also seemed to proclaim that Jillian felt a new sense of power with her advanced age. This little sister was now bigger and starting school again. Unlike the first grader of last year, she would return as a veteran.

The differences between Ben's and Jillian's experiences thus far became suddenly apparent to me. At seven years of age, Ben had been frustrated and discontented in first grade in the new experimental Spanish immersion school. He'd been one of the oldest of his first-grade peers and could barely read and write, partly because everything was in Spanish. Jillian, in contrast, was now excitedly beginning second grade, was reading well above grade level, and was socially well-connected at school. Both children at the age of seven were enthusiastic about learning about their world, but Ben had rapidly become stale on the business of school, whereas Jillian was enjoying it and thriving on it.

As parents, our experiences between the three years were strikingly different as well. When Ben was seven, I hadn't even met the school's gifted and talented teacher and was unfamiliar with the details of current research, assessment, and the broad range of gifted and talented children and gifted education issues. Every situation was new and unfamiliar and required exhaustive reading and hours of discussion.

As I looked back at those early years, we were pioneers in a territory that we would gradually settle into and be comfortable with. The going was rough and difficult at first, but now we could travel the trails with confidence and relative ease because we had worn them smooth with hours of reading, research, discussion, and thought.

We had by now traded the bare essentials of pioneer life (including our shotgun for quick defense) for the more permanent fixtures and methods of well-settled farmers. No longer did we fear the potential danger of wildcat teachers or black bear administrators. Instead, we had acquired new respect and skills that enabled us to live together with our children's educators productively. We shared resources. We solved problems together. We settled in and worked the land by peaceful means using all of our previous experience. We acquired new knowledge with which to nurture our children. We were now beginning to reap the harvest from the earlier seeds we had sown. We had cultivated long-term partnerships. Teachers and administrators had by now become trusted friends. Jillian was clearly benefiting from our early pioneer-like parenting and learning experiences as we had advocated for Ben during his younger years.

The first week of second grade, just after Labor Day, I received a friendly e-mail from Tina Jansen, the gifted and talented teacher. By this time, we were on a first-name basis.

*How's your garden doing with the recent rain? It
sure is welcome after the dry spell of last month.*

*I've been in touch with Chendra Dorsher and
think it would be good to get together soon next
week to talk about Jillian's education needs this
year. Let me know when a good time to meet
would be, if you agree.*

~ Tina

P.S. Say hi to the kids for me!

With a combination of trepidation and high hopes, my
heart jumped a small hurdle in my chest. I assumed that Tina
and Jillian's new teacher would want to follow up on the conversations that we'd had two years previously about Jillian's grade
placement. Last spring and over the summer, Tina had alluded
to the possibility of accelerating Jillian in September. After
forwarding Tina's e-mail to Brian at work, he wrote back that he
wasn't sure exactly what her e-mail meant. His reply contained
several questions: "What do they want? Why so early? What is
their agenda?"

I responded to Tina's e-mail.

*How about next Tuesday? We will both be avail-
able that day; just name a time. It will give us the
weekend to think about where we're at, too.
Thanks, Tina, for keeping tabs on Jillian!*

~ Wendy

Brian and I discussed Jillian's situation over the weekend,
but for only a fraction of the time that we'd spent on a similar
discussion for Ben three years earlier. This time, we were familiar with the system and its players, had a positive track record,
and had a solid, well-earned trust in our gut feelings and logical
reasoning. We came to several conclusions.

We could not forget that Jillian was an exceptionally gifted child. Besides her intellectual gifts, she was socially adept and had already demonstrated the drive, skills, and attention span of a studious learner. She craved knowledge and understanding well beyond what a regular classroom situation could offer. She was outgoing, friendly, spirited, physically coordinated, and tall for her age as well—all this despite her young chronological age, as compared to others in her class.

Like Ben, Jillian was beginning the new year in an ideal classroom situation—one of two second-third multi-grade classrooms. She could be accelerated and still remain with her teacher, Mrs. Dorsher, and classmates but still be allowed to move up to the homogenous third-grade group for the language arts and math core content areas. She would have the full support of Mrs. Dorsher and the other team teacher, Mr. Lund, as well as the continued relationship and support from Tina Jansen.

Brian and I decided we'd be open-minded to whatever Tina and Mrs. Dorsher had to propose, not knowing for sure if it meant a whole-grade skip or not. "It would be ideal if Jillian could just be a third grader for language arts and math, and then just be a second grader for the rest of the day," I confided to Brian that Monday night before our meeting.

He quickly replied, "But that's *exactly* what the multi-grade classroom could be for her."

Brian and I were prepared and ready for our meeting on Tuesday afternoon at 3:30. By 4:00, we all agreed that Jillian would be in with the third graders for language arts and math but would remain in her second-grade gifted pullout group. The second-grade group had eight children as opposed to the third-grade group's 13. Jillian would still have a familiar and cohesive group to belong to, and Tina said she had big plans for this particular group. At the end of third grade, children are reassessed for gifted services again, creating a slightly different set of children at the fourth-grade level, with some continuing and some new participants. Jillian would have to readjust to this group next year in fourth grade anyhow, so why not give her one more year of stability with her second-grade gifted and talented pullout classmates?

I should note that the gifted teacher was essential in this whole process. Tina Jansen knew Jillian and kept her in her thoughts throughout the school year and summer months, as she did the other gifted children. She initiated her own discussions with the principal and classroom teacher. She scheduled our meeting early in the year to help Jillian make the transition earlier and therefore easier. Mrs. Dorsher, Jillian's teacher, made it clear that she couldn't possibly claim to know Jillian well enough this early in the year to even begin to make such recommendations for her as an individual.

"And," Mrs. Dorsher said to me afterwards, before Brian and I left the school building, "I've known Tina for a long time. We talked about Jillian, and I have a great deal of trust in her judgment."

Don't assume that the teachers just came right out and said, "Let's accelerate Jillian." They didn't. Mrs. Dorsher and Tina Jansen both gave us a clear picture of what second-grade content was like (repetitious of first grade with the least amount of new material introduced when compared to any other elementary grade), as well as their professional opinions on how the second- and third-grade content would match up to Jillian's abilities. We gave them our opinions, as parents, on Jillian's drive and skill levels. Not until the group had a balanced discussion about Jillian's ability, her present level of knowledge, and her social and emotional maturity and readiness did the staff ask what we as parents wanted.

"It is up to you," Tina said.

"What do you want for Jillian this year?" Mrs. Dorsher followed.

I gently nudged Brian's arm with my hand from under the table and made eye contact with him. I smiled.

Brian returned the gazes of the teachers and stated clearly and confidently, "We think she should be in third grade. She *needs* to be." And with that, it was decided.

Magic and Mysteries Revealed

As it is with every story, circumstances change, and what appears to be magic at first has a less mystical explanation later. This story began when our children were born. At the beginning of our journey, I was enthusiastic, naïve, and inexperienced. Now that I have acquired the magical spectacles of 20/20 hindsight, I want to share some of my thoughts as I look back on my children's early school years. Those thoughts include my personal involvement and volunteer work in gifted issues, people I met in the process, and the way some things have changed or evolved in the schools that my children attended. I will also comment about the various choices we made.

One aspect I did not emphasize as strongly as I might have in my story is the extent that my husband and I became involved in the school community through volunteering and how that involvement impacted our children's situations. In addition to my volunteering in the daily classroom activities such as language arts time, math activity day, class fieldtrips, and parties, Brian and I were involved in several other ways.

Brian was a member of the Taft Primary School Site Council, a policy council that included the principal, teachers, staff, and parents. In addition to discussion and influencing a wide variety of school policies, he aided Mr. Swenson, the principal, in building renovation project planning. The relationship that developed between the two men resulted in additional mutual respect and friendship and provided opportunity for better communication with a man who had a great deal of influence on the educational opportunities of our children.

When Jillian was in kindergarten and Ben was in second grade, I was the chairperson of the local chapter of The Minnesota

Council for the Gifted and Talented. This council, called MCGT, is a statewide organization of parents, educators, administrators, and professional people who live or work with gifted children and are interested in their education and well-being. For two years, I organized and scheduled programs, discussions, classes, children's activities, and social gatherings for the families of gifted children in our city. I spoke as a gifted parent representative at a teacher in-service on intellectual diversity. I was also a parent member of two school district committees. At the state level, I was active as a volunteer with MCGT at their annual state conference and participated as a panel speaker in several MCGT seminars.

Because of my experiences and involvement with gifted and talented issues, phone calls to MCGT were often referred to me from parents, the school, and from acquaintances. I responded confidentially to parents' concerns about their own gifted children. I assisted parents whose families were new to the area by informing them of various school opportunities.

By actively volunteering in the classroom and by becoming active in the local and state gifted and talented advocacy organizations, I continued to learn about gifted children while helping others. Because of these experiences, my husband and I were able to develop mutually respectful relationships with those who had an influence in our children's education that we might not otherwise have had.

Certainly, not all families can afford the time to be involved as much as we were, particularly when both parents work full-time jobs. However, even a small amount of volunteering can build the kind of trust that leads to communication and problem solving in a team effort with school staff.

With our involvement, some people became especially important to us. As the years progressed, Tina Jansen became a dear friend to our whole family, especially to Jillian and me. Little did I know when we first met that she'd had only had six years of experience specifically as a teacher for gifted and talented.

However, she had previously taught for many years, including six years in multi-grade classrooms. She proved to be a quick and thorough learner, and her expertise improved with every year. As I got to know her better, I came to recognize and appreciate her passion, talent, skill, and sound judgment when dealing with gifted and talented students. Our family owes many of our children's early successes to her thoughtful guidance.

Although Mary Vanasek appears only briefly in this account, her powerful and positive presence became increasingly important as Ben and Jillian grew into teenagers. She reached out on her own, beyond her grade-specific duties as Gifted and Talented Teacher and Counselor, to meet and get to know both children. She had met with Ben to do some math assessment in first grade when we first realized that our situation was more complicated than we had expected. This tiny seed became the foundation of a mutually respectful friendship with him. When Jillian was in sixth grade, Mary reinforced previous connections with her by sending a thoughtful get-well card when Jillian was experiencing some serious mental health issues. Both of our children love and trust Mary and do not hesitate to seek out her guidance when necessary. She has helped our family out in tough times and has advocated on issues regarding scheduling and classes for both children. She has been honest, supportive, and encouraging to me and Brian as parents and adult peers. Nothing can substitute for positive, trusting relationships when it comes to asking for and receiving help for one's gifted children.

At the time, some of the events surrounding Ben's and Jillian's grade accelerations seemed almost magical to us. Ben's combination second-third-grade teacher, Melissa Margoles, recognized his readiness to accelerate after only eight weeks of school. Looking back now, I realize that she must have had discussions with Tina Jansen and Mr. Swenson regarding Ben's situation. The true magic was demonstrated by an insightful teacher and the behind-the-scenes teamwork of staff, all of whom had the power and desire to make a difference in Ben's life.

The same can be said about Jillian's situation when her acceleration was discussed after only two weeks of school. In this case, the magic came from a decision by the staff of the gifted and talented program to carefully document the progress of students being considered for acceleration. By conscientiously monitoring the progress of all of the identified gifted and talented students, the gifted and talented teachers can prescribe interventions or accommodations for each student as needed. The result is an approach of proactive planning rather than reactive efforts.

Magic can never account for the vision and persistence of a school district and an administration committed to making unique educational opportunities work for children. In the beginning, we were overwhelmed by the perceived lack of ability of the Spanish immersion school to meet Ben's needs. We felt we had no other choice but to remove him from the school. Now, years later, that school and its administration have blossomed and matured. The school is running full tilt with kindergarten through sixth grade. It has a strong, highly qualified principal, as well as a modern, upgraded, permanent facility. I am unaware of any children experiencing a full-grade acceleration there. However, I do know of two students who were given a single-subject acceleration, moving one and two years ahead in math. And the school currently has its own dedicated gifted and talented teacher. While it may not be capable of meeting the needs of every highly gifted and talented student, the Spanish immersion school has now become a strong choice for many.

Finally, our hopes for our children would not have become a reality if we had not had an exceptional public school system and citywide community. Our city, a first ring suburb of Minneapolis/St. Paul, has a long tradition of academic excellence, including gifted services, which began in the early 1970s, and continues with an International Baccalaureate program established at our high school in 2001 and in our elementary schools in 2007.[16] Recognition and action regarding gifted children and gifted education is supported in every tier in the school system. The entire community, including the schools, government, and religious organizations, strive to create an environment that is supportive of every child. Our city was the pilot community for the program "Children First," which is now used in hundreds of communities across the United States. It is within this greater environment of community support that the gifted and talented program thrives.

I cannot emphasize strongly enough that although gifted children have many similarities, every child is born with his or her own unique character, personality, and innate abilities, and each family has a different set of life experiences. Whole-grade acceleration, as we did with Ben and Jillian, will not be the best option for every child.

There is great diversity within the gifted population. Not all gifted children operate at the same level, have the same interests, or are equally gifted in all areas. Just as there is great variation within the general population, there is also great variation within the gifted and talented population. Schools are realizing more and more that each child has unique strengths and weaknesses and that an education program should be tailored, wherever possible, to the child's intellect, achievement level, and learning readiness. Social and emotional development should be considered as well.

Ben and Jillian scored in the highly gifted or exceptionally gifted range, so the need for acceleration for them was greater than for a child in the beginning range of gifted. Children at even higher levels might not be able to find an education to meet their needs in any type of school but might benefit from home schooling or individualized tutoring instead.

When a gifted child needs more than what the average classroom offers, parents and teachers should consider a variety of educational strategies. These methods can be used by themselves or in combination with others; they can be used temporarily or consistently for many years. They can be implemented by the school administration, the regular classroom teacher, the gifted specialist, or by parents at home. Strategies include early entrance to kindergarten or first grade, whole-grade acceleration (grade skipping), single-subject acceleration, curriculum compacting, continuous progress, clustering, pullout programs, dual or concurrent enrollment, post-secondary programs, Advanced Placement (AP) classes, the International Baccalaureate (IB) Program, College in the School, mentorships, and full- or part-time home schooling.

There are many resources in which to learn more about educational strategies for gifted children. In her book *Stand Up for Your Gifted Child*, Joan Franklin Smutny gives a concise and useful overview of some of the educational strategies listed above for gifted children in the chapter "Understanding Gifted Education." You'll find this book and others listed in the Resources section of this book. A book that explains all of the gifted options, while also noting what research results indicate for each option, is *Re-Forming Gifted Education: How Parents and Teachers Can Match the Program to the Child* by Karen Rogers, Ph.D. This book also contains other valuable information for parents and teachers, such as lists of Talent Search programs, competitions, magazines, and reading lists appropriate for gifted children, as well as advice on how to approach the schools to request modifications to the usual education plan for your child.

Some options like Advanced Placement (AP) classes, the International Baccalaureate (IB) Program, College in the School, and some mentorships are geared specifically for secondary students. You can check with your high school administration or guidance counselor or search online for more information on these programs.

If you are new to gifted education and public schools, your child's school situation may seem confusing and at times mysterious. I urge you to read up on gifted and talented education and to look for parent advocacy groups where you can meet others with similar concerns. Most importantly, I encourage you to cultivate relationships and find an advocate within the school system for your family, and make your own magic happen.

 Epilogue

The story, of course, continues. Children grow and change, and not always in pleasing or comfortable ways. Like many families, we have discovered that there can be unexpected and disorienting bumps in the road and that seldom are there easy answers or simple solutions for a child in the complex process of growing up. Nevertheless, our family continues to learn and grow from the experiences.

At eight years of age, when fully immersed in fourth grade, Jillian proclaimed, "My favorite thing about fourth grade is the homework!" She was, and still is, extremely punctual when it comes to completing homework assignments. In addition to the regular classroom, she was in the pullout program for gifted and talented students and for math challenge students. She enjoyed playing violin in the school's chamber symphony for the more experienced string players. On Saturdays, she participated in the Minneapolis Children's Theater. She was energetic and enthusiastic about her diverse activities and the new friendships she was developing.

In the last few months of fourth grade, however, her optimistic spirit diminished alarmingly. She began to isolate herself from friends and family and experienced daily debilitating stomachaches and headaches. Perhaps most disturbing of all were her sudden emotional outbursts of anger or sadness. By fifth grade, my husband and I were convinced that she was exhibiting symptoms of some sort of emotional problem, and

Jillian began seeing a therapist on a regular basis. She was diagnosed with general anxiety disorder and depression, and she worked with her therapist to understand her emotions and the reasons behind her physical symptoms.

By November of sixth grade, and at the age of only 10, Jillian was severely depressed with suicidal ideation. She was admitted to an afternoon treatment program for children with affective mental health disorders. After assessment, the program director determined that Jillian was too mature in many ways for their grade school program and advised that she be placed with the 12- to 14-year-olds in the middle school program. It turned out to be good advice. For the next several months, half of Jillian's school day was spent in day treatment. It seems that even in her emotional problems, she was years ahead of her age peers; her depression was more like that of teens or young adults.[17]

Two and a half years after Jillian first exhibited symptoms of anxiety and depression, she appears to be fully recovered. Individual counseling; independent behavioral, group, and recreational therapy; medication; support from her school district administration, principals, teachers, and family; and the passage of time have allowed her to grow and mature. She no longer takes any medication, and she only sees her therapist on an as-needed basis.

For now, Jillian has come full circle. She is 12 years old and in eighth grade. To ease some of the external time pressures, she has dropped private violin lessons, though she still plays with the school orchestra. She enjoys swimming on the school's competitive swim team and has resumed playing low-level competition summer soccer. She has made many new friends, especially girls.

Jillian is in accelerated math and language arts classes and enjoys rigorous expectations from her geography, science, and German teachers. She has challenging, compassionate, humorous teachers who support her intellectual, social, and emotional growth. Two teachers have become especially important mentors for her, in academics as well as personally.

When Jillian was in first grade, I remember that I feared she might one day adopt a "submissive, quiet, don't-attract-too-much-attention mentality" by the time she reached junior high. Now, I can safely say that, after those few dark years of anxiety and depression, she has burst forth out into a bright world of social and intellectual independence. The strength of her sense of self defies my earlier doubts. Nevertheless, her father and I do not take for granted her gentle laugh, a phone call to one of her friends, or a quiet, restful night of sleep. We are deeply grateful that she is healthy and happy and is enjoying friends and activities at school. For now, we can rest easy—that is, until her next developmental challenge.

Fourth grade was a major milestone year for Ben as well. In contrast to Jillian, Ben had to make a huge adjustment to classroom and homework assignments. Perhaps because things had always been so easy for him and he'd never had to do homework or study, he exhibited poor personal time management and rarely completed his assignments on time. His procrastination hung over his conscience like a dark shadow looming over his bed each night—it nagged at him to the point of tears—until he finally asked for help from us and his teacher, Mr. Wilson. That was the beginning of learning good study habits and building self-confidence in his abilities to complete assignments on time. By fifth grade, Ben had learned how to manage his time effectively, much to his and our relief. For the most part, he continues to have good work habits, although when it comes to long-term assignments, the ghost of procrastination is ever present.

When Ben was in the sixth grade, he enjoyed his time with his classmates and his teachers. He woke at 6:30 A.M. each day on many cold, dark, and wintry Minnesota mornings. Along with five other sixth graders, he rode the bus to the junior high for a seventh-grade accelerated math class. He looked forward to it every day, not only because he enjoyed the math class, but because he also got to ride the bus with some seventh-grade friends who had been in Mr. Wilson's mixed-grade class.

Ben is now a 15-year-old sophomore in high school. When students from the three elementary schools combined in the junior high school, his circle of friends grew dramatically. He kept some of his old friends but discovered other friends from the Spanish immersion school. In eighth grade, he joined the cross-country running team, which has a history of attracting some of the brightest students, both boys and girls, in the school. He found kindred spirits there, too. The friendships he developed in junior high continue to be some of his closest and most supportive in high school. Like any teenager, his social circle is ever changing as he chooses which friendships to hold onto and which ones to let go.

In seventh grade, Ben traded the accordion he'd been playing since third grade for playing percussion in the school band. In tenth grade, he traded band class for computer programming I and II. Next year, he's returning to band since he's recognized how much he misses belonging in a musical social group. He continues to take challenging math classes, and this year is no exception. He is in an AP calculus class, his favorite class this year not only because of the subject, but also because of an inspiring, caring, talented math teacher. However, the A's he has earned in math have not always come easily for him. Only with determination, help from teachers and peers, and at times tears of frustration has he come to understand the ever-more-complex concepts. He's developed a solid work ethic, nurtures supporting relationships in study groups, and has attained a sense of self-direction and pride in his work. Our biggest concern as parents at this point is that he not put too much pressure on himself. Achieving a balance is an ongoing theme of discussion in our household when it comes to friendships, personal creativity, physical activity, schoolwork, and family time. And lately, with college just around the corner, following your heart's desire has become a new priority for dinner table talks.

When Ben first set his sights on learning division in the first grade, we never imagined that his abilities and self-determination would eventually lead him to enroll in a college calculus class at the age of 15. Likewise, when he hid under the science table in nursery school, I couldn't foresee the socially brave and confident young man he is today.

These days, we enjoy a small sigh of relief since both of our children are happy with their lives and their education. We are pleased that they have found appropriate challenge and are well on their way to lifelong learning, productive careers, and satisfying adult lives. They continue to help us gain a new understanding of infinity and zebra stripes.

Resources

Organizations

Several national organizations are available for anyone interested in improving the lives of gifted children. If you are looking for a statewide organization closer to home, check with the National Association for Gifted Children, with which many state organizations are affiliated.

National Association for Gifted Children (NAGC)
1701 L Street NW, Suite 550
Washington, DC 20036
(202) 785-4268
www.nagc.org

The National Association for Gifted Children (NAGC) is a non-profit organization that receives no government funding. It is supported solely by membership dues, an annual convention, sale of publications, and donations. NAGC is an organization of parents, teachers, educators, other professionals, and community leaders who unite to address the unique needs of children and youth with demonstrated gifts and talents, as well as those children who may be able to develop their talent potential with appropriate educational experiences. NAGC develops policies and practices that encourage and respond to the diverse expressions of gifts and talents in children and youth from all cultures, racial and ethnic backgrounds, and socioeconomic groups. NAGC supports and engages in research and program development, staff development, advocacy, communication, and collaboration with other organizations and agencies which strive to improve the quality of education for all students. Membership includes a choice between *Gifted Child Quarterly* and *Parenting for High Potential* magazines, plus discounts on NAGC materials, other publications, and conferences. Members enjoy the opportunity to network within specific interest groups, from Arts and Creativity to Early Childhood, and Special Schools and Programs. The organization's website is a tremendous resource for parents and teachers and includes links to about 40 state associations for gifted children.

The Association for the Gifted (TAG)
The Council for Exceptional Children (CEC)
1920 Association Drive
Redstone, VA 20191-1589
(888) 232-7733 (888-CDC-SPED)
www.cectag.org

The Association for the Gifted (TAG) was organized as a division of The Council for Exceptional Children in 1958. TAG plays a major part in helping both professionals and parents work more effectively with one of our most precious resources: the gifted child. Visit the website for information on such topics as: Questions from Parents about Gifted Children, Interesting Internet Sites, Legislative Issues, Membership Information, and articles from the *Journal for the Education of the Gifted*.

Supporting Emotional Needs of Gifted (SENG)
P.O. Box 6550
Scottsdale, AZ 85261
www.sengifted.org

Many schools, communities, and organizations focus on the intellectual needs of gifted individuals. Supporting Emotional Needs of Gifted (SENG) seeks to inform gifted individuals, their families, and the professionals who work with them about the unique social and emotional needs of gifted persons as well, which are often misunderstood or ignored. SENG, a nonprofit organization, was formed in 1981 to provide guidance, information, resources, and a forum to communicate about raising and educating high-ability children. Today SENG has expanded its goals to focus not only on gifted children, but also on gifted adults. It supports programs that foster the mental health and social competence necessary for gifted individuals to be free to choose ways to develop and express their abilities and talents fully. The mission of SENG is to empower families and communities to influence more positively and effectively the development of giftedness in those individuals entrusted to their care. By underwriting and providing education, research, theory building, and staff development, SENG promotes environments where gifted individuals can develop positive self-esteem, utilize their talents, and thrive.

The Gifted Child Society
www.gifted.org

On this website, you can explore what The Gifted Child Society is actually *doing*—not just saying—like offering conferences, Saturday morning classes, workshops, training, etc. There is a separate section for a parents' forum, as well as a teachers' forum. The Gifted Child Society is a nonprofit organization that was founded in 1957 by parents in New Jersey to further the cause of gifted children. Goals include educational enrichment and support services, assistance to parents, professional training, and a greater effort to win public recognition and acceptance of the special needs of bright and talented children. Since 1957, the Society has served more than 60,000 children and their families. In 1975, the U.S. Department of Education named it a national demonstration model.

Minnesota Council for the Gifted and Talented (MCGT)
5701 Normandale Road, Suite 345
Edina, MN 55424
(952) 848-4906
www.mcgt.net

As one example of a statewide association (there are about 40 listed as links on the NAGC website), MCGT provides information, literature, and referral services, publishes a bi-monthly newsletter, conducts topical seminars, sponsors an annual state conference with special children's programs, promotes advocacy at all levels for gifted and talented children, is active in legislative efforts on behalf of kids in collaboration with the Minnesota Educators of the Gifted and Talented, and participates in a national network through its affiliation with NACG and other organizations. Chapters throughout the state offer opportunities for local activities.

Internet Websites

Websites are constantly changing, so listed below are a few different sites that seem to be stable, of high quality, and that offer a broad scope of resources with plenty of detail within. Note that each site contains links to other gifted sites as well. Some of the sites are solid educational institutions offering educational strategies and information. Think of these recommendations as doorways leading to multiple sources of information and networking on gifted and talented-related issues.

Hoagies' Gifted Page
www.hoagiesgifted.org
> This website offers a tremendous variety of information and resources, with topics including: "Gifted 101" and "Gifted 102," Characteristics of Gifted, Identification, Testing and Assessment, Highly Gifted, Traditional School, Home Schooling, Programs, Special Needs, Parenting Support, Special Topics, FAQs, Shopping Guide, and Success Stories. In additional to content for parents, there are sections specifically for educators, teens, and children, as well as an extensive list of resources. Want to find "it"? Chances are, Hoagies has got it.

Davidson Institute for Talent Development (DITD)
www.ditd.org
> The Davidson Institute focuses on the needs of highly and profoundly gifted young people. In addition to numerous articles and resources on its website, it has a Young Scholars Program, Summer Institutes, and a Davidson Fellows Scholarship Program. DITD GT-CyberSource links readers to an extremely large collection of information for and about gifted students.

Gifted Development Center (GDC)

www.gifteddevelopment.com

Since 1979, the Gifted Development Center (GDC), located in Denver, Colorado, has served as a resource center for developmentally advanced children and their parents, as well as for gifted individuals of all ages. It offers in-depth assessment, counseling, consulting services, and innovative materials. GDC also provides true expertise and experience with gifted issues and the unique perspective of looking at giftedness from the inside—as advanced awareness and emotional intensity—in addition to the challenge that these individuals experience as often being out-of-sync with the rest of the world. This organization has helped more than 4,000 families better understand and nurture their children's development. Parents have learned about their own giftedness as well. GDC publishes a journal on adult giftedness, *Advanced Development*, which brings greater self-awareness to parents.

GT World

www.gtworld.org

GT World was formed by a group of "parents in the trenches" who met on the TAGFAM (Talented and Gifted Families) Internet site (www.tagfam.org), and in 1997 decided to form their own organization. It began with GT-Families, which was followed quickly by GT-Adults, GT-Special and GT-Spec-Home for people dealing with the double whammy of giftedness and learning disability, and GT-Talk. Topics to click on include a variety of electronic mailing lists for onsite discussions, definitions, testing information, articles, books, and links. The GT Testing Information is extremely useful—a treasure chest of information all in one easy-to-read spot for parents who are trying to understand the complexities of testing or assessment. Also, the GT Links is a thoroughly comprehensive guide to websites for gifted issues.

Education Program for Gifted Youth (EPGY)

www.epgy.stanford.edu

The Education Program for Gifted Youth is an ongoing research project at Stanford University dedicated to developing computer-based multimedia courses in mathematics, physics, English, computer programming, and other subjects and making these available to students of high ability in elementary and secondary school. EPGY endeavors to provide students with advanced courses regardless of where they live, do so without requiring them to leave their normal school environment, individualize instruction and accommodate individual differences in student learning, and allow students to progress at their own pace and to accelerate their education. This reputable program is worth investigating as an alternative means of individualized instruction, whether it is within the traditional or home school environment.

International Baccalaureate (IB) Organization
www.ibo.org

The International Baccalaureate (IB) organization, founded in 1968, is a nonprofit educational foundation based in Geneva, Switzerland, and is gaining in recognition and implementation in public schools across the United States. As a particularly challenging and stimulating curriculum with a global focus, it offers to schools three programs: the Diploma Program, the Middle Years Program, and the Primary Years Program. There are 1,888 authorized IB world schools in 124 countries (as of November 2006). It grew out of international schools' efforts as early as 1924 to establish a common curriculum and university entry credential. The schools were also motivated by an idealistic vision. They hoped that critical thinking and exposure to a variety of points of view would encourage intercultural understanding by young people. They concentrated on the last two years of school before university studies in order to build a curriculum that would lead to what they called a "baccalaureate," administered in any country, recognized by universities everywhere.

The IB Mission Statement: "The International Baccalaureate Organization aims to develop inquiring, knowledgeable and caring young people who help to create a better and more peaceful world through intercultural understanding and respect. To this end the IBO works with schools, governments and international organizations to develop challenging programmes of international education and rigorous assessment. These programmes encourage students across the world to become active, compassionate and lifelong learners who understand that other people, with their differences, can also be right."

Search Institute
www.search-institute.org

Search Institute is an independent, nonprofit, nonsectarian organization whose mission is to advance the well-being of adolescents and children by generating knowledge and promoting its application. To accomplish this mission, the institute generates, synthesizes, and communicates new knowledge, convenes organizational and community leaders, and works with state and national organizations. At the heart of the institute's work is the framework of 40 developmental assets, which are positive experiences, relationships, opportunities, and personal qualities that young people need to grow up healthy, caring, and responsible. Created in 1990, the framework is grounded in research on child and adolescent development, risk prevention, and resiliency. Surveys of more than one million sixth- through twelfth-grade youth in communities across the United States consistently show that young people who experience more of these assets are more likely to make healthy choices and avoid a wide range of high-risk behaviors. The relative absence of these assets in the lives of young people in every community studied has prompted hundreds of communities to mobilize on behalf of young people.

Children First
www.children-first.org

Children First is a call to individuals, families, and organizations to reclaim their responsibility for young people and provide the guidance, support, and attention that young people need to be successful. Children First is a philosophy, not a program. This philosophy was first adopted by five partners in St. Louis Park, Minnesota, and has rapidly spread to other individuals and organizations. It was the first local initiative to take Search Institute's groundbreaking youth development research and transform it into community action. Since Children First began in 1993, hundreds of communities across the nation have started similar initiatives. For more information on other initiatives, visit Search Institute's website.

National Research Center on the Gifted and Talented
www.gifted.uconn.edu/nrcgt.html.
The National Research Center on the Gifted and Talented, funded by the Jacob K. Javits Gifted and Talented Students Education Act, is a nationwide cooperative of researchers, practitioners, policy makers, and others. The NRC/GT offers a wide assortment of free and cost-recovery only research-based materials for educators and parents (several translated into Spanish). More information is available at http://www.gifted.uconn.edu/nrcgt.html.

Books and Recordings

The number and variety of high quality books addressing gifted issues is astounding compared to a decade ago. Included in this section are books about parenting and schooling, as well as the leading educational research and books geared specifically for gifted children. There is also a list of narrative non-fiction books—personal accounts by parents of gifted children—more stories to add to your vicarious parenting experiences. This sampling of books and recordings is only a small fraction of the excellent books available. Please refer to the websites previously listed to find extensive reference listings.

Parenting Issues
A Parent's Guide to Gifted Children. James T. Webb, Janet L. Gore, Edward A. Amend, & Arlene DeVries. (2007). Scottsdale, AZ: Great Potential Press. A comprehensive guide to gifted children, with examples and advice. This book addresses typical parenting concerns, but within the specific context of gifted children. Written for parents in a common sense voice, it includes hard research and developmental psychology that brings breadth and depth to each topic. Three chapters are especially relevant for gifted children. These are: Chapter 6. Intensity, Perfectionism, and Stress; Chapter 7. Idealism, Unhappiness, and Depression; and

Chapter 12. Children Who Are Twice-Exceptional. Read all the way through, or quickly find the advice you need on a single topic.

Freeing Families from Perfection. Thomas Greenspon. (2001). Minneapolis, MN: Free Spirit Publishing. Perfectionism is not the same as striving for high quality in all that you do. Perfectionists are more motivated by fear of failure than by desire for success. Anyone who thinks they know what perfectionism is, or who wonders if they or a member of their family suffer from perfectionism, or is just plain curious about why people do the things they do will find this fairly short book enlightening. Information is provided clearly without offering confusing technical definitions or jargon. It is interesting, well-written, and informative, with a strong focus on working within the family to help one another and provide support. Greenspon offers different scenarios for discussion, varying according to age of children, and also lists resources for more information on most of the topics covered in the book.

Gifted Grown-Ups: The Mixed Blessings of Extraordinary Potential. Marylou Kelly Streznewski. (1999). New York: John Wiley & Sons. This book will help parents of gifted children understand and acknowledge their own giftedness. It includes characteristics, excerpts from interviews of 100 gifted grownups ages 18 to 90, and discussion of critical issues that face gifted grownups.

Problem Child or Quirky Kid?: A Common Sense Guide. Rita & John Sommers-Flanagan. (2002). Minneapolis, MN: Free Spirit Publishing. This book gives parents the advice, reassurance, and practical knowledge they need to help their child and themselves. It covers common childhood problems and suggests remedies for parents to try at home. It also explains the world of mental professionals and when it might be appropriate to take advantage of professional help.

Stand Up for Your Gifted Child: How to Make the Most of Kids' Strengths at School and at Home. Joan Franklin Smutny. (2001). Minneapolis, MN: Free Spirit Publishing. Reading this book is comparable to having one of the nation's leading experts on gifted education as a personal consultant on call 24 hours a day. A practical guide to help parents advocate for their child, it includes how to recognize a child's giftedness, understanding his or her problems at school, and how to figure out a school district's gifted education policies. The suggestions promote collaboration between parents and school rather than an adversarial approach. All of the tools and resources parents need for effective advocacy are provided, including resource lists, and real-life examples are used as illustrations.

The Survival Guide for Parents of Gifted Kids: How to Understand, Live with, and Stick Up for Your Gifted Child (rev. ed.). Sally Yahnke Walker. (2002). Minneapolis, MN: Free Spirit Publishing. This book is a great place to turn for facts, insights, strategies, and sound advice about what giftedness is (and isn't), how kids are identified, how to prevent perfectionism, when to get help, how to advocate for your child's education, and more.

You Know Your Child Is Gifted When...: A Beginner's Guide to Life on the Bright Side. Judy Galbraith. (2000). Minneapolis, MN: Free Spirit Publishing. An easy read, this book is compact both in content and size and is great either as a basic reference or as a refresher. Humorous cartoons blend with solid information on giftedness—its characteristics, challenges, and joys. Each chapter features a tell-tale characteristic: advanced intellectual ability, verbal proficiency, curiosity, creativity, high energy, focus, passion, intensity, logical thinking, sensitivity, and sense of humor. First-person stories from parents who have been there offer reassurance and insights. Galbraith discusses what sets gifted kids apart, how you can support your child's unique abilities, how to strengthen parenting skills, and more. Excellent resources are included.

Education Issues

Creative Home Schooling: A Practical Resource for Smart Families. Lisa Rivero. (2002). Scottsdale, AZ: Great Potential Press. This is an excellent resource for anyone with gifted kids. Rivero offers basic information about the traits and needs of gifted children and explains how home schooling can help to meet many of these needs. Even if you don't home school, this book gives insight into the process of educating a gifted young person. Especially noteworthy is the "Big Ideas" concept of unit studies, which fits very well with the intense, insatiable knowledge quest of many gifted learners. The book also includes a superb list of resources.

Crossover Children: A Sourcebook for Helping Children Who Are Gifted and Learning Disabled (2nd ed.). Marlene Bireley. (1995). Reston, VA: The Council for Exceptional Children. From more than 35 years of experience as a teacher, psychologist, and university professor, Bireley has written this very readable "how to do it" book for parents, regular classroom teachers, teachers of learning disabled/gifted and talented students, school psychologists, counselors, and administrators. It offers guidelines for a better education and therefore better opportunities for this group of children. This is a rich resource that provides specific strategies, recommendations for academic interventions, and enrichment activities to help twice-exceptional children (who may also be ADD) to control impulsivity, increase attention, enhance memory, improve social skills, and develop a positive self-concept. Sections of the book deal with educational planning and programming for gifted/learning disabled children, behavior and social interventions, academic intervention, academic enrichment, and some things to consider as crossover children grow up. Complete appendices include resources, organizations, computer programs, and a bibliography.

The Iowa Acceleration Scale, 2nd Edition: A Guide to Whole-Grade Acceleration K-8. Susan Assouline, Nicholas Colangelo, Ann Lupkowski-Shoplik, & Jonathan Lipscomb. (2003). Scottsdale, AZ: Great Potential Press. Making decisions regarding whole-grade acceleration can be challenging. Although this tool would typically be utilized by a professional educator and a child study team, which would include a child's parents, it also provides a clear window of insight for any parent who is agonizing over whole-grade acceleration. Developed and tested by the Belin-Blank Center at The University of Iowa, the IAS ensures that acceleration decisions are systematic, thoughtful, well-reasoned, and defensible. The IAS is used in 50 states, Canada, and

Australia. Feedback from years of widespread use has resulted in a second edition of this unique, systematic, and objective guide to considering and implementing academic acceleration.

Jane and Johnny Love Math: Recognizing and Encouraging Mathematical Talent in Elementary Students. A Guidebook for Educators and Parents. Ann E. Lupkowski & Susan G. Assouline. (1992). New York: Trillium Press. Inspired by the Study of Mathematically Precocious Youth (SMPY) for junior and senior high school students at Johns Hopkins University, the authors have adapted the model of instruction for students younger than 12. A comprehensive approach is presented concerning identifying and educationally facilitating the needs of mathematically gifted students. Topics include diagnostic testing, followed by prescriptive instruction, curriculum, and materials; case studies of talented youths; guidelines for a useful educational assessment; and long-term planning. Fifty pages of extensive and useful resources include an appendix, glossary, and reference list. This is an inspirational guide, whether you follow it to the letter, choose to apply bits and pieces, or use it to delve deeper into the literature to answer your questions about educating the young math wiz in your life.

Losing Our Minds: Gifted Children Left Behind. Deborah Ruf. (2005). Scottsdale, AZ: Great Potential Press. Based on behaviors and developmental milestone data, as well as test data, Ruf classifies gifted children into five levels. This fascinating book gives parents and educators a reference guide as a basis for comparing their own gifted children or students with other children. Educational implications arise depending upon the child's level of giftedness, and the book discusses these implications, as well as the difficulties that many schools have in adjusting to meet the various levels.

A Love for Learning: Motivation and the Gifted Child. Carol Strip Whitney, with Gretchen Hirsch. (2007). Scottsdale, AZ: Great Potential Press. This is a well-written book that rings true to what turns gifted and talented kids on or off. Because gifted children are susceptible to many de-motivating factors, which can lead to academic underachievement and even depression, parents need a guidebook like this that describes concepts and techniques that can nurture and spark motivation. The focus is on how families and schools can foster a physical, intellectual, and social-emotional environment that is naturally exciting as well as comforting for gifted children. Based in solid research and practical experiences, it includes chapter summaries and carefully selected anecdotes. An excellent resource for new parents, as well as professionals.

Re-Forming Gifted Education: How Parents and Teachers Can Match the Program to the Child. Karen B. Rogers. (2002). Scottsdale, AZ: Great Potential Press. This book describes various types of gifted children and options for school enrichment and acceleration, including the effectiveness of each option, according to the research. Rogers shows parents and teachers practical ways to design ongoing programs that best meet the needs of bright children. The book is comprehensive, well-organized, and child-centered, with the target audience being parents and guardians of gifted kids. It combines non-threatening quizzes, illustrative case studies, exhaustive research, and several helpful inventories to create a variety of "advocacy templates" for parents and other adults charged with the responsibility of advocating for gifted students during their K-12 school years.

Teaching Gifted Kids in the Regular Classroom: Strategies and Techniques Every Teacher Can Use to Meet the Academic Needs of the Gifted and Talented (rev. ed.). Susan Winebrenner. (2000). Minneapolis, MN: Free Spirit Publishing. This is an excellent guide to meeting the learning needs of gifted students in the mixed-abilities classroom—without losing control, causing resentment, or spending hours preparing extra materials. Each chapter presents a specific strategy with step-by-step instructions for implementation, from curriculum compacting to creating challenging tasks from regular content. This guide is practical and applicable in the traditional school setting, as well as home schooling or tutoring.

Teaching Young Gifted Children in the Regular Classroom: Identifying, Nurturing, and Challenging Ages 4-9. Joan Franklin Smutny, Sally Yahnke Walker, Elizabeth Meckstroth, & Marjorie Lisovskis. (1997). Minneapolis, MN: Free Spirit Publishing. With its special emphasis on the early years of primary school, this guide is inspirational as well as practical. Each chapter is devoted to topics including identifying gifted children, creating a learning environment, compacting the curriculum, extending learning, promoting creativity in the curriculum, cluster grouping, comparative learning, and finding and supporting giftedness in diverse populations. Extensive references and resources including tests for identifying young gifted children, resources for teachers, sources for gifted and talented educators, a bibliography, reproducible pages, websites, and books.

Social, Emotional, and Special Needs

Counseling the Gifted and Talented. Linda Kreger Silverman (Ed.). (1993). Denver, CO: Love Publishing. Because gifted children are cognitively complex and emotionally intense, counseling techniques need modification for them. A developmental model and specific strategies are discussed to provide a program of prevention rather than remediation. This book includes valuable bibliographies, resources for counseling and assessment, and lists of books for young readers. Parents are a child's first counselor, and this book makes it so much easier to "do the job" for gifted children. Characteristics of giftedness, emotional aspects, overexcitabilities, special needs, peers, home, school, even multi-cultural and gender issues are dealt with in this comprehensive volume. Counselors, psychologists, and other professionals who deal with gifted children should read this book and keep it as reference on their shelf close at hand.

"Mellow Out," They Say. If I Only Could: Intensities and Sensitivities of the Young and Bright. Michael Piechowski. (2006). Madison, WI: Yunasa Books. Piechowski's long-awaited book on emotional intelligence resonates with the real voices of gifted adolescents who speak with insight and passion about the realities of their emotional lives. It is an important book

that elucidates what bright teenagers think. Drawn into thematic order using responses from open-ended questionnaires, this book adds to the literature on giftedness by going beneath the surface of high achievement into development.

Misdiagnosis and Dual Diagnoses of Gifted Children and Adults: ADHD, Bipolar, OCD, Asperger's, Depression, and Other Disorders. James T. Webb, Edward R. Amend, Nadia E. Webb, Jean Goerss, Paul Beljan, & F. Richard Olenchak. (2006). Scottsdale, AZ: Great Potential Press. Our brightest, most creative children and adults are often misdiagnosed with behavioral and emotional disorders such as ADHD, Oppositional-Defiant Disorder, Bipolar Disorder, Obsessive-Compulsive Disosrder, or Asperger's Disorder. Many receive unneeded medication and inappropriate counseling as a result. Physicians, psychologists, and counselors are often unaware of characteristics of gifted children and adults that mimic pathological diagnoses. Six nationally prominent healthcare professionals describe ways parents and professionals can distinguish between gifted behaviors and pathological behaviors. Fifty percent of the royalties from this book go directly to Supporting Emotional Needs of Gifted (SENG), a nonprofit organization dedicated to gifted children and adults.

Smart Boys: Talent, Manhood, and the Search for Meaning. Barbara Kerr & Sanford Cohn. (2001). Scottsdale, AZ: Gifted Psychology Press. Using current research and personal interviews, the authors explore why many of our brightest boys and young men underachieve in school and fail to reach their full potential in the world of work, and why they often have problems with depression in adolescence or their adult years. This book includes suggestions and insights for parents and teachers. It is a much-needed and comprehensive look at an often-overlooked gifted population. It also includes many anecdotes and is very readable.

Smart Girls: A New Psychology of Girls, Women, and Giftedness (rev. ed.). Barbara Kerr. (1997). Scottsdale, AZ: Gifted Psychology Press. Talented, gifted girls often disguise their potential in adolescence and adulthood. This book provides answers and practical advice to parents, teachers, and policy-makers about ways to help gifted girls continue to grow and succeed. Topics include bright beginnings, barriers to achievement, adolescence, self-actualization, guiding gifted girls, eminent women, gifted minority girls, and gifted college women. It is important reading for every parent of bright daughters, and it is suitable for the girls themselves as well.

Social/Emotional Needs of Gifted and Talented: What Do We Know? Maureen Neihart, Sally M. Reis, Nancy M. Robinson, & Sidney M. Moon (Eds.). (2002). Waco, TX: Prufrock Press. In this book, a publication of NAGC, leading scholars comprehensively summarize several decades' worth of the best research on the social and emotional characteristics of, and issues faced by, gifted children and adolescents. They offer what they learned from the research they examined. The book's 24 chapters explore underachievement, perfectionism, acceleration, peer pressure, depression, delinquency, risk and resilience, and social acceptance among gifted students. Also addressed are specific populations within the gifted community, such as the special concerns of girls and of boys, students with disabilities or ADHD, the creatively gifted, and gifted children who are gay, lesbian, or bisexual. Each chapter reviews and presents research relevant to the topic, with the authors carefully distinguishing fact from fiction regarding the social-emotional and psychological characteristics of gifted children.

Research and Scholarship

Exceptionally Gifted Children (2nd ed.). Miraca Gross. (2003). Oxford: Routledge Books. The first edition of this book, published in 1993, introduced 15 remarkable children in Australia—some of the most gifted young people ever studied, and traced their paths through school, exploring their academic achievements (and in some cases enforced underachievement), their emotional development, their social relationships, and their family relationships and upbringings. This new edition reviews these early years but also follows the young people over the subsequent 10 years into adulthood. The study reveals the ongoing negative academic and social effects of prolonged underachievement and social isolation imposed on gifted children by inappropriate curriculum and class placement and shows clearly the long-lasting benefits of thoughtfully planned individual educational programs. The young adults of this study speak out and show how what happened in school has influenced and still influences many aspects of their lives. Gross provides a clear, practical blueprint for teachers and parents who recognize the special learning needs of gifted children and seek to respond effectively.

Once Upon a Mind: The Stories and Scholars of Gifted Child Education. James R. Delisle. (2000). Orlando, FL: Harcourt Brace. This book is a comprehensive and useful introduction to the field of gifted education, its history, and curriculum. It is intermingled with interviews and stories that highlight the lives and works of educators and researchers who have devoted their time and energy to gifted children, as well as anecdotes from gifted kids and their parents who describe their experiences and struggles with an education system that does not always meet their needs. It includes many interactive questions and related resources. Delisle hopes that this book will be "the beginning of an intellectual journey, rather than the entire trek." It is an excellent reference book.

The Young Gifted Child: Potential and Promise. An Anthology. Joan Franklin Smutny (Ed.). (1998). Cresskill, NJ: Hampton Press. This is a fine collection of articles about gifted children ages one through seven that is practical, informative, wide-ranging, and comprehensive in its scope.

For Kids

The Gifted Kids' Survival Guide: A Teen Handbook (rev. ed.). Judy Galbraith & Jim Delisle. (2001). Minneapolis, MN: Free Spirit Publishing. Written with the help of hundreds of gifted teenagers, this is the ultimate guide to surviving and thriving in a world that doesn't always value, support, or understand high ability. The book is a must for gifted teens, their parents, teachers, counselors, and anyone who cares about smart, creative, curious kids.

The Gifted Kids' Survival Guide for Ages 10 and Under (rev. ed.). Judy Galbraith & Jim Delisle. (1998). Minneapolis, MN: Free Spirit Publishing. Hundreds of gifted youngsters contributed to the original book and to this revision. Their input reflects an honest, candid discussion about their unique concerns. Written for smart, creative kids, this is a must-read for young gifted children and their parents. It can also be a great read-along with a gifted child that can open up discussion in non-threatening ways about school, friends, teasing, and being "different."

Vivaldi's Ring of Mystery: A Tale of Venice and Violins. 45 minutes. Available now in CD and sometimes DVD format, this tale from the well-known Classical Kids series introduces children to the music of Vivaldi by following the story of Katarina, a pupil at the school for orphans in Venice where Vivaldi taught for most of his life. A gondolier befriends Katarina and shows her around Venice at Carnival time. When Katarina runs into trouble with a mysterious violin, Vivaldi tells her the story of his own life. The story is accompanied by selections of Vivaldi's most famous works, including "The Four Seasons." The acting, singing, and chamber music are all superb. This and other tapes in the series are highly imaginative, historically accurate, and appropriate for all ages. Other titles in the series include: "Beethoven Lives Upstairs," "Hallelujah Handel!" "Mozart's Magic Fantasy," "Mozart's Magnificent Voyage," "Mr. Bach Comes to Call," "Tchaikovsky Discovers America," and "Song of the Unicorn."

Memoirs: Personal Stories from Parents

A Case of Brilliance. Rebecca Lange Hein. (2002). New York: Xlibris. This book sprang from Hein's awakening to her role as a parent and teacher of two profoundly gifted children. She and her husband began this work knowing only that their children were "bright." IQ testing and the counseling that followed led both parents to revolutionize their approach to childrearing and home schooling. Hein's book is written with passion, not only about recognizing her children's potential, but also about coming to terms with her past and present as an extraordinary gifted adult. Read more at www.rebeccahein.com.

Genius in Residence. Audrey Grost. (1970). Upper Saddle River, NJ: Prentice Hall. This book offers an honest and sometimes humorous, well-written, and remarkably objective account of the author's highly gifted son and the reactions of their family and community. Lifestyle changes, coping mechanisms, and relationships with school at all levels and professional personnel are described. Your child may or may not attend college as a 10-year-old as Grost's son did, but you're sure to relate to this mother's experience in many other ways. Don't let the 1970 copyright fool you, either. Many issues with parenting gifted children are timeless. This book is currently out of print and may be difficult to get a hold of, but very much worth the effort.

Raisin' Brains: Surviving My Smart Gifted Family. Karen Isaacson. (2002). Scottsdale, AZ: Great Potential Press. Isaacson reveals herself as both a hilarious writer and gifted parent of an eclectic but endearing gifted and creative family. She refers not only to her five children, but to her extended family of aunts, uncles, and particularly her mother. The parenting advice she gives through Erma Bombeck-like humor and stories is universal. She achieves success at conveying the realities of gifted children who come in all combinations of gifts or "weirdness."

Success Stories in Gifted Education. Hoagies's Gifted Education Page has a series of more than a dozen personal success stories in e-book form available on its website at www.hoagiesgifted.org/success_stories.htm. Story topics include home schooling, testing, twice-exceptional children, exceptionally gifted, Montessori, early entrance, etc., and include children of all ages. It is interesting and easy to access.

 Endnotes

1 Generally, experts refer to various ranges of giftedness. For example, children with IQ scores of 130 to 145 are often referred to as Moderately Gifted, children with IQ scores of 145 to 160 as Highly Gifted, those with scores of 160 to 180 as Extremely Gifted, and those with IQ scores above 180 as Profoundly Gifted. These terms are, of course, only generalizations, yet they are useful starting points for educational planning and for understanding many of a child's behaviors. Dr. Deborah Ruf's book *Losing Our Minds: Gifted Children Left Behind* describes many of the behavioral characteristics of children at various IQ levels.

2 Some gifted children need less sleep than other children; others seem to need more. For more information, see *A Parent's Guide to Gifted Children* (Webb, Gore, Amend, & DeVries) and *Misdiagnosis and Dual Diagnoses of Gifted Children and Adults* (Webb, Amend, Webb, Goerss, Beljan, & Olenchak), which are listed in the Resources section of this book.

3 As Drs. Barbara Kerr and Sanford Cohn note in their book *Smart Boys: Talent, Manhood, and the Search for Meaning*, gifted boys are often more sensitive and androgynous, and frequently they don't like the macho activities of other boys.

4 The ceiling effect is now more widely recognized, and there are newer tests and modifications of older test that allow psychologists with an understanding of gifted children to assess upper levels of ability.

5   At the time that Wendy had her son tested, a few psychologists were still using the Stanford-Binet, L-M, but it is seldom used nowadays, especially since it is out of print and difficult to find. These days, almost all child psychologists use a revision of that test, the new Stanford-Binet, V, published in 2006, which will work with gifted youngsters when the test administrator understands how to interpret the test for gifted children. Dr. Deborah Ruf provides an excellent explanation of the new tests in her book *Losing Our Minds: Gifted Children Left Behind.* She explains how the newer tests can be used successfully with gifted children when the psychologist has some knowledge of attributes of gifted children, including an understanding that these children are often asynchronous—that is, they may be greatly advanced in one or two areas but yet appear average or even have a learning disability in other areas.

6   Some experts have noticed a "bump'" on the bell curve at around 160 to 170 IQ. In other words, there is a higher frequency of children in this IQ range than would be expected by a normal bell curve. Experts say more research is needed.

7   It is common for gifted children to be strong-willed. They love to argue a point and can easily get into power struggles with adults with whom they disagree.

8   Gifted children are often more androgynous in their interests and friendships than other children.

9   Jillian's attempt to explain a scientific concept like evolution is not unusual for gifted children. These children often question belief systems and may try to come up with their own understanding of the world and the universe.

10 Highly gifted children are often unusually sensitive to problems of characters in stories, whether in books or other media, and may become quite frightened, sad, or emotional.

11 Gifted children, with varying levels of giftedness, are often early in reaching developmental milestones such as talking in sentences or reading on their own. The variety of their interests and abilities in the different levels is astonishing. Many gifted children teach

themselves to read and do math calculations, for example, before entering kindergarten. Dr. Karen Rogers, in her book *Re-Forming Gifted Education: How Parents and Teachers Can Match the Program to the Child*, explains many different educational options for gifted children in schools—options that don't cost the school anything extra, except that it must be flexible. For example, a third grader could go across the hall to fifth grade during math time, if he is already doing math at a fifth-grade level. Another gifted child who finishes work easily and early may work on an individual project in an area that interests her. For more examples, see the gifted options described in Rogers' book.

12 For more information, see *A Parent's Guide to Gifted Children* by Dr. James Webb, Janet Gore, Dr. Edward Amend, and Arlene DeVries and *Losing Our Minds: Gifted Children Left Behind* by Dr. Deborah Ruf.

13 In previous decades, the Gesell test was used widely by districts to determine "readiness," but since gifted children develop in an asynchronous manner, this test is not appropriate for determining their school readiness. Like the Vineland inventory, the Gesell measures skills such as socialization, independence, and motor skills, but it does little to estimate or measure intellectual ability. Schools sometimes—mistakenly—refuse to provide advanced educational opportunities simply because a child's motor skills, such as the ability to draw or use scissors, are lagging behind. This, of course, is not appropriate. Bright children need challenge to stay engaged in learning.

14 A newer and more thorough and systematic way now exists to decide on early entrance or grade skipping. Dr. Susan Assouline and her colleagues at the Belin-Blank Center developed *The Iowa Acceleration Scale* (now in its second edition), which guides a child study team through all of the factors related to successful whole-grade acceleration. Research with *The Iowa Acceleration Scale* has generally shown that the earlier the acceleration, the better; thus, accelerating to first grade would be better than waiting another year. Although a two month trial period is fine when accelerating a child, a decision to accelerate need not be irrevocable. Reversing the decision does not seem to have harmful consequences.

15 Challenging traditions, particularly those that make no sense to them, is another of the common traits of gifted children. When they have more experience living in the world, they can better accept traditions as commonly accepted behaviors. For more information, see *A Parent's Guide to Gifted Children* (Webb, Gore, Amend, & DeVries).

16 Information about the IB program, including its website address, is listed in the Resources section of this book.

17 Depression is not uncommon in gifted children. Some of it is that they are more sensitive to problems in the world and are sad that things like war, hunger, and poverty affect so many. With their idealism, they see how things could or should be, and when they see how the world and people fall short of their ideals, they become saddened and even depressed. For more about depression in gifted young people, see the chapter on idealism and depression in *A Parent's Guide to Gifted Children* (Webb, Gore, Amend, & DeVries).

About the Author

Wendy Skinner lives a stone's throw from Minneapolis, Minnesota, with her husband, two gifted children, a dog, a gerbil, and a goldfish. She earned her B.A. in Elementary Education from the University of Northern Colorado. As the quintessential career substitute teacher, Wendy has taught nearly a decade in bilingual, Spanish immersion, special education, and regular classrooms in every grade and nearly every subject. She also teaches writing part-time in a nontraditional fifth/sixth-grade mixed classroom. When she is not teaching or advocating on behalf of gifted children and their families, she spends her time with her family, writing, and selling cut flowers at a farmers' market during the summer.